D1372219

FROM FAITH TO FAITH

Essays on Old Testament Literature

———————

FROM FAITH TO FAITH

Essays on Old Testament Literature

B. DAVIE NAPIER

ASSOCIATE PROFESSOR OF OLD TESTAMENT,
YALE UNIVERSITY

Harper & Brothers, Publishers

NEW YORK

FROM FAITH TO FAITH

Copyright, 1955, by Harper & Brothers ©
Printed in the United States of America

*All rights in this book are reserved.
No part of the book may be used or reproduced
in any manner whatsoever without written permission except in the case of brief quotations
embodied in critical articles and reviews. For
information address Harper & Brothers
49 East 33rd Street, New York 16, N. Y.*

Library of Congress catalog card number: 55-8525

To
MY MOTHER AND FATHER
Christian Missionaries in China, 1905-1930
parents who taught
the biblical faith
by living it

Contents

Preface

Through the long centuries and the moving history that produced the Old Testament, the faith of the continuing community of Israel shaped and interpreted the several types of Israel's literature. In the five chapters of this book I have selected and discussed outstanding examples of Old Testament myth, legend, history, prophecy and law in an effort to show that common theological presuppositions underlie all of these varying literary types, and that they must be read and understood as speaking from faith to faith. From faith the literature in all of its types came into being. To faith it is all addressed. From myth to law, Old Testament literature deals centrally with the same concepts of faith, such concepts as Creation, Sin, Judgment, Covenant and Redemption. As different from one another as are these varied literary types, *as literature,* they are remarkably unified in the common history and faith of the community of Israel.

Chapters might have been included on selections from the wisdom and devotional literature. But as a type of canonical literature, Israelite wisdom remained relatively peripheral and always more personal than communal in character; and the Psalter, to which occasional reference has been made, is self-evidently in a faith-to-faith category of expression. It is hardly necessary to add that what I have written is certainly not intended as a substitute for an introduction to, a history of, a commentary upon, or a theology of the Old Testament.

These chapters, then, are an effort to interpret certain fundamental aspects of the faith of Israel as they appear in common in varied types of her literature. But I have tried first to assess the quality of faith with empathy, from within the community in which the faith was created and nurtured. In this effort I have been most materially helped by my reading of Johannes Pedersen, H. Wheeler Robinson and Gerhard von Rad, some of whose works are cited in the essays. I have tried not to complicate the discussion unduly. Some will no doubt feel that I have succeeded too well. Matters of controversy (in which Old Testament study abounds) have been sometimes ignored and often passed over lightly. Footnotes, except in the last chapter, have been held to a minimum.

No book *about* the Bible is a substitute for the biblical literature itself. This is not offered in lieu of the texts with which it deals. If there is any value in what I have written here, it is to be realized only insofar as these chapters are employed as a companion to the Old Testament.

Quotations from the Bible follow, as a rule, the Revised Standard Version, Thomas Nelson and Sons, publishers, to whom grateful acknowledgment is made. On rare occasions I have given other renderings of the Hebrew text; italics are always mine; and I have often substituted the Hebrew divine name, Yahweh, for the R.S.V.'s "the Lord," a term, for most of us, loaded with connotations foreign to the ancient Israelite. Where the Hebrew and English versification differs, I have followed the English versions.

Gratitude is also expressed for permission to use Chapter V, which originally appeared in a slightly different form in *Interpretation*, Vol. VII, No. 4 (October, 1953), pp. 404 ff.

I am indebted to Mr. Everett Sims; Dean B. W. Anderson of Drew Theological Seminary; Professor Millar Burrows, my one-time teacher and now esteemed senior colleague; Professor Franklin W. Young, until recently an associate of mine at Yale and now Professor of New Testament at the Episcopal

Theological Seminary in Austin, Texas; and Professor Claude Welch of Yale. All of these have read and criticized parts of this book in manuscript. None, of course, may in any way be held responsible for its shortcomings.

B. DAVIE NAPIER

Heidelberg, Germany
February 12, 1955

Introduction

Until their retirement some years ago, my mother and father were missionaries in China, where I was born and reared. Both are musical and both were, and still are, quite literally singing Christians. Gospel hymns were a part of my environment; and I still remember snatches of songs that I have heard, so far as I know, only from them.

One of these starts, as I recall, "I'm a little old-fashioned, I know" and elsewhere declares, "I believe that the Bible is true, though the critics have torn it apart."

Certainly I knew nothing then of the vast grounds for the hymn-writer's protest, but later in the decade of the thirties I joined, incipiently at the level of a graduate student, the ranks of the same critics and with some real enthusiasm learned and cultivated the techniques of "tearing apart" the biblical literature.

With what astonishing swiftness the religious temper virtually of the whole Protestant world has changed. The positions are in a partial sense reversed. It is in fact the very position assailed in the song which is now "a little old-fashioned." For now there is no more prominent and significant sign of our religious times than the "rediscovery" of the Bible. In the main this recovery—perhaps a better term—involves no annulment, no abrogation of the principles and insights of the era of "tearing apart"; but it does imply, in sum, a radical change in interpretation.

Old Testament scholarship continued well into the twentieth century employing the techniques of the nineteenth century; and the nineteenth century was for the Old Testament an era of protracted and major surgery. To carry the analogy of surgery further, nineteenth-century scholars performed a series of exceedingly thorough exploratory operations, checked all arteries to the source, neatly classified according to their lights all living tissue and as neatly set aside all intrusive and extraneous items. At the turn of the century, they handed the Old Testament, now a thoroughly objectivized patient, into the next hundred years.

One could wish that the scholars' change of role had taken place then. But younger professionals in the field of Old Testament studies were themselves trained in the presence of so much surgery that they were, to use an inelegant phrase, scalpel happy. They could not or would not put down the knife; and when the patient, the Old Testament, was understandably a little slow in convalescing and taking the theological field of battle, they placed him again on the table and continued in exploratory surgery. With truth the analogy can be carried to extreme terms in saying that some among the scholar-surgeons performed in such a way as to suggest that they regarded their task not as an operation but as an autopsy.

Norman Snaith, a British scholar, wrote not many years ago:

There are limits beyond which literary analysis cannot be pressed without doing more harm than good. Even the good order of JEDP may corrupt the scholarly world. We have been so very energetic in isolating each from the other, and even within each, in separating stratum from stratum, that we have tended to forget that there might be method in the madness which so thoroughly dovetailed them in together. Perhaps, after all, that madness was divine.[1]

A. Trends in Old Testament Interpretation

This quotation sharply points up one of the significant tendencies in Old Testament interpretation. The work of editors is seen as not merely editorial but in fact creative, presenting a unity often transcending the multiple and at points contradictory sources employed. S. H. Hooke, in his little volume on Genesis entitled *In the Beginning*, quotes from a letter written to him by an unnamed scholar. Hooke obviously quotes with approval:

I hold that Genesis is one book . . . written from many sources, not three, and these sources were in a form or language which had to be completely remodelled by the author of the book in order to make them intelligible. That being so, it is impossible to say whether there were in existence collections of stories for the author to use or not, though we may guess that it is very probable.[2]

While the majority of scholars in Europe and America would be unwilling to dismiss so casually the results of nineteenth-century literary analysis, certainly a growing number would agree that the sense of unity achieved in Genesis, or in the Hexateuch (Genesis–Joshua), or for that matter in the entire Old Testament, is impressive despite the diversity of sources from which it was created. Which is simply to say that there is a growing disposition to regard that madness, if not always as divine, at least as purposive.

Another closely related current trend in Old Testament interpretation is sharply to discount the older notions of disparity between priest and prophet. This older view is characterized in the following blast against the priests from a living American scholar of great repute:

They [the priests] were wholly unconscious of having sanctified the external, obliterated from religion both the ethical ideals of

Amos and the tender emotions of Hosea, and reduced the universal Creator to the stature of an inflexible despot. . . . Regulation took the place of spontaneity, discipline stifled freedom, solemnity displaced joyousness.[3]

Such a statement as this is today sharply challenged. The prophetic and the legal, the prophet and the priest, are not seen as consistently and inimically opposed in the Old Testament. I have elaborated on this trend in Chapter V.

A third trend which ought to be briefly mentioned has to do with the point of emphasis in the comparative study of Old Testament religion with that of Israel's neighbors. If in the past stress has been placed on similarities, the tendency is now marked to recognize beyond what is common the essential and significant difference. Let me cite two illustrations. The stories of Genesis 1-11 show a striking resemblance at points to stories of human origin circulating in other ancient Near Eastern civilizations. This discovery led to a common view of all of them, including the biblical myths, as primarily etiological, that is, as stories primarily explaining in terms of origin certain persistent and universal questions. But against and beyond the similarities, the Genesis myths reveal in spite of latent primitivisms a far more refined and consistently articulated theology. The study of comparative religion has led fruitfully beyond the discovery of mere similarity to a better understanding of the unique quality of biblical revelation.

Finally, we note the tendency to interpret the Old Testament in terms of its major, its persistently recurrent, themes. If in the few preceding generations we have been concerned or even obsessed with the meaningful task of discovering the *process*, literary and historical, by which it came to be, we are now gratefully in a position to see the Old Testament not simply as process, but as completed process, not as a series of sequential parts but as a unified whole.

To speak of Old Testament unity implies absolutely no deprecation or repudiation of the insights gained in an understanding of the process of the Bible's becoming. To speak so does, I think, demand a high measure of participation in its story, and an effort to understand it first in its own terms—to grasp the Old Testament's own fundamental assertion that its story from beginning to end is the account of the historical action of God seeking the reconciliation of man and God, the human and the divine, the creature and the Creator.

In this perspective, the Old Testament conveys the impression of coherent unity—a unity achieved in the central themes and presuppositions of the community of Israel. There are at least six of them, which I can only list here, but which, in one way or another, I have tried to point up in the chapters that follow.

1. A consistent and startlingly immediate faith in creation.

2. A second, and all are closely interlinked and interdependent, the nature of human sinfulness, interpreted always in part against the presuppositions of the creation faith.

3. Divine judgment, historical judgment, consistent, on the one hand, in its punitive quality with the concept of God-as-Creator-Judge but, on the other hand, transcended in the main by the concept of God-as-Redeemer into judgment not merely punitive but ultimately itself redemptive in character and purpose.

4. The covenant faith, exemplified in Abraham, in Moses and the Exodus, in the nation Israel, in the Remnant, and in the Messiah or the Servant.

5. The theme of redemption, present from the beginning, and always the fundamental motive in the interpretation of history.

6. And finally, the theme of consummation, the faith in consummation—consummation, the necessary ultimate extension of faith affirming the absolute sovereignty of God, declaring not so intentionally precisely *how* it shall be established but simply that it shall be.

> The wolf shall dwell with the lamb, and the leopard shall
> lie down with the kid, and the calf and the lion and the
> fatling together, and a little child shall lead them. . . . They
> shall not hurt or destroy in all my holy mountain; for the
> earth shall be full of the knowledge of the Lord as the waters
> cover the sea.
>
> [Isa. 11:6, 9]

B. The Nature and Technique of Interpretation

The interpretation of the Old Testament (and indeed of
any literature) is both a technique and an art embracing a
much broader perspective than is sometimes recognized. The
usual assumption in interpretation is that one takes a given
passage or text and by detailed analysis, careful study and
imaginative but disciplined meditation determines as accurately and in such detail as possible all of the meaning
expressed and implied therein.

In this sense, interpretation is a task with clearly defined
limits. The given passage, now explained and interpreted, is
a completed unit and may be left behind by the student for
a new and different unit. But this, obviously, is an inadequate
function of interpretation. What of the whole from which
the passage is taken? Is not the whole in very fact the
synthesis of the parts, of the details? Is it not then a necessary function of interpretation to set the interpreted part
back into the whole again in order that the whole may better
be understood?

Take, in brief example, the Call of Isaiah.[4] One immerses
oneself in a study of the account—and the passage (Isa. 6)
will profitably bear long and deep immersion—not simply
to know and understand what the prophet experienced in
his call and how he himself regarded his difficult and perplexing charge, but to know and understand also how his

experience and his interpretation of his charge affected his total ministry.

And this begins to set Old Testament study into nearly limitless terms. Isaiah's writing is studied by passages and chapters better to understand Isaiah; but Isaiah must be understood for what Isaiah can do to enlighten the whole movement of Hebrew prophecy. An understanding of Hebrew prophecy is essential for an understanding of the larger whole, the Old Testament. And the ultimate end is of course a better understanding of the Judeo-Christian faith.

All of this is to say of Old Testament study and interpretation that it is an effort better to see the whole through the elucidation, understanding and synthesis of the details. And this is one, but only one, of the two major approaches.

The second approach, sometimes overlooked or implicitly denied as a function of interpretation, is from the opposite direction—from the general to the particular. If it is true that the whole is seen as a synthesis of the details, it is also true that the details can be fully understood only in the light of the total context. If the whole yields its meaning only from the details, it is equally true that the details can be fully comprehended only in the light of broad principles, sweeping and basic presuppositions derived from a general understanding of the whole.

The study of any significant literature, fully conceived, is always thus dialectical and so conceived it has no limits. The details will be utilized unceasingly in the explanation of the whole, and the broad principles of the whole will in turn be applied to the details. If this is the serious intention of the Bible reader, many of the common errors in biblical understanding will be avoided. Interpretation so conceived prohibits on its own definition the lifting of a text out of context. The text's function is to enlighten the context; and the context must be understood if the text is to be explained.

I am quite aware that this view of Old Testament study and interpretation strongly presupposes a considerable measure of unity in Old Testament literature. It is not of such a kind or degree as to rob the various writers of their individuality, to say nothing of their fallibility. Rather, it is a unity derived from principles of community and canon; from the memory of the community of Israel; and from Israel's understanding of its past and its present (and its future) as time and event given ultimate meaning only in terms of critical divine activity for critical divine purposes.

C. The Sources of Genesis

By the turn of the last century, a three-source hypothesis (J, E and P) in Genesis was thought to be in its major lines and by its major proponents at least as well-established as the Copernican theory. There were then and have been until the present differences of opinion as to identification by documents of certain passages, sentences, phrases, and even words; and the precise lines of the hypothesis are still with some scholars a point of energetic debate. But among scholars who would class themselves as supporters of the Graf-Wellhausen scheme,[5] there *is* wide accord—and they are unquestionably a majority.

Within their ranks, however, there have appeared some significant variations affecting source analysis in Genesis. Before the turn of the century the J source had been divided into two different strands. Eissfeldt, in 1922, proposed the symbol L (for "lay" source) for that strand of J dealing with popular legends and myths and reflecting a more primitive social and theological background. The bulk of Eissfeldt's L source occurs in Genesis and coincides with much that is ascribed by the older scheme to J.

A somewhat similar variation is Pfeiffer's proposal of a source in Genesis which he designates S, for Seir, the region comprising Edom to the south of Palestine. It is a source which Pfeiffer sees as considerably less extensive than Eissfeldt's L source, comprising about a dozen stories in Genesis only. It is, however, a more radical departure from the conventional three-source hypothesis, for it is seen as totally at variance in form and thought with J and as betraying a vigorous hostility to Israel and its religion. It is the editorial work of an Edomite who, by skillful selection and arrangement, stamps the source with his own philosophy of history, namely, that "cultural progress is accompanied by increased wickedness and unhappiness."

While some scattered support has been given to both of these modifications of the three-source hypothesis in Genesis, a third recent and more serious modification has as yet gained few followers. Rudolph and Volz, two German scholars, launched in the 1930's a frontal attack on the E document. It is, they maintained, a myth sincerely but erroneously created by the Graf-Wellhausen school of critics. As a "source" E is quite incoherent and must, in fact, be seen for the most part as mere supplements to J.

In the early decades of this century, Hermann Gunkel, while certainly no opponent of the established hypothesis, led a movement representing especially in Genesis a marked shift of emphasis. Gunkel analyzed the Genesis material primarily according to type, not document. Upon such criteria as literary form, the nature of the tradition, the social and theological concepts underlying and the apparent motivation of the story, Gunkel classified the myths and legends of Genesis. In introducing form analysis, Gunkel unquestionably has been influential in the more recent criticism of the standard multiple-source hypothesis among scholars in Germany, Great Britain, and especially Scandinavia.

Along more conservative lines, a distinguished German scholar, Martin Noth, has recently proposed and presented evidence for a more ancient source than J (he does not commit himself as to whether it was an oral or written source) underlying both J and E and utilized by both. He calls the source G for the German term *Grundlage,* "basic source."

By all odds the most radical departure from the Graf-Wellhausen school of criticism is among scholars in the Scandinavian countries loosely designated by the term "Uppsala School." In Professor I. Engnell three major lines of Scandinavian Old Testament scholarship converge, coming from Pedersen, Mowinckel and Nyberg. All four of these reject in one way or another the validity of the older multiple-source theories. Engnell sees no adequate criteria for distinguishing between so-called J and E. He places strong emphasis upon cult and oral tradition; and he predicates meaningful unity only in extended sections of the Old Testament: the Tetrateuch, Genesis–Numbers, is a unity characterized by the pervading priestly point of view dominant in the entire section; and Deuteronomy–II Kings is a second major unit reflecting chiefly the perspective of the Deuteronomic point of view.

It would be well to conclude this brief survey of some of the most significant recent theories in source analysis with the judgment of Aage Bentzen.[6] It is of first importance, he states, that we understand the "import of the 'old school,' so that continuity in science can be seen and the new points of view get their true background. Our criticism of them [the new points of view], and our attempts at a solution of our own we must then view in the light of the insecurity of the present situation, as attempts, not as final words. We are living in an age where new thories are about to be born."

I. MYTH

In the Beginning: Genesis 1-11

The earth is full of thy creatures . . .
These all look to thee,
   to give them their food in due season.
When thou givest to them, they gather it up;
   when thou openest thy hand, they are filled with
     good things.
When thou hidest thy face, they are dismayed;
   when thou takest away their breath, they die
   and return to their dust.
When thou sendest forth thy Spirit, they are created;
   and thou renewest the face of the ground.

Ps. 104:24c, 27-30

This is what the community of Israel believed. This became her fundamental article of faith, and in this mature expression of her creation faith, Israel denies that God having created then withdrew from his creation to let it proceed on its own laws and regulations. Israel never thought of God as creator alone but always as creator-sustainer, creator-preserver.

This is what Israel believed. This is an expression of her matured creation faith.

A. In the Image of God (Gen. 1:1-2:4a)

In the stories of Gen. 1-11, Israel has preserved and cherished what she deems to be the essential prelude to her own particular story beginning with Abraham. The life of the people Israel has meaning only against a background of cosmic sweep and universal scope. Israel understands her own history only in relation to God's creation and preservation of all life everywhere. She interprets her place and function in history in terms of a universally broken relationship between creator and creature, God and man. Gen. 1-11 defines the universal condition that explains Israel's particular history.

The Old Testament opens on the note of creation, in a story (Gen. 1:1-2:4a) which did not come to its final form until after the Babylonian exile in the sixth century b.c. It is a story of creation patterned after similar non-Israelite stories yet shaped distinctively and unmistakably by the character and mind of Israel.[1] This is a fully matured, priestly declaration of faith, which distills in and for fifth-century Israel the essence of that community's belief about the relationship between man and God, and about the nature of man as a creature of God.

The creation story of Gen. 1 is, then, an appropriate opening to Israel's scripture because it reflects a matured understanding of the faith and history of the community. It is appropriate, too, because in phenomenally brief compass it defines and illumines some of the central affirmations of that continuing community. One of these affirmations is reflected in the eight occurrences of the phrase, "God said . . ." (vv. 3, 6, 9, 11, 14, 20, 24, 26). The story expresses, accepts as valid, and reconfirms Israel's faith that the word of God, the divinely spoken *Word* is never merely descriptive: it is a Word possessing and releasing power, effecting—bringing to pass, causing to be—that to which the Word refers, or that which the Word describes. The story at once gives expression to and further defines the historically conditioned faith of Israel: it was God's Word through Moses that wrought her physical redemption from slavery in Egypt; it was the same dynamic Word, centuries later, that brought judgment against the sinful nation; and the same Word again that effected the return and restoration of Israel.

Here is the dynamic divine Word in its ultimate projection. We quote Gen. 1:1-3 in a translation and form more precisely conveying the sense of the text:[2]

In the beginning of God's creating of the heavens and the earth—when the earth was waste and void, when darkness was upon the face of the deep, and when the spirit of God was brooding over the face of the waters—then God said, "Let there be light." *And there was light!*

The Word of God calls into being that which was not! And the magnificently articulated story unfolds, projected from a corporate imagination informed to be sure by cruder stories of creation but motivated and controlled by the sense of the powerful divine Word in history.

The story reflects and is a commentary upon Israel's faith that the decisive factor in her history, and all history, is the creative and dynamic Word of God. It also affirms the essential goodness of creation, again with an emphasis in repetition: seven times—of every item of creation except the second—the responsive refrain occurs, "God saw that it was good" (vv. 4, 10, 12, 18, 21, 25, 31, the last, "very good"). This too reflects a central and consistent quality of the faith of Israel, a faith which the psalmists express in joyful praise:

Bless the Lord, O my soul! . . .
Thou didst set the earth on its foundations,
　so that it should never be shaken. . . .
Thou makest springs gush forth in the valleys; . . .
they give drink to every beast of the field; . . .

Thou dost cause the grass to grow for the cattle,
    and plants for man to cultivate,
that he may bring forth food from the earth,
    and wine to gladden the heart of man, . . .
    and bread to strengthen man's heart.

[Ps. 104:1, 5, 10, 11, 14, 15]

The good creation joyously acclaimed in the community is expressed and given ultimate confirmation in the story of creation. One of the psalmists recalls gratefully the goodness of man in his creation:

When I look at thy heavens, the work of thy fingers,
    the moon and the stars which thou hast established;
what is man that thou art mindful of him,
    and the son of man that thou dost care for him?
Yet thou hast made him little less than God,
    and dost crown him with glory and honor.

[Ps. 8:3-5]

The history of Israel shows nowhere the slightest inclinations to asceticism: the full richness of a good creation is for man's enjoyment, and he accepts the satisfactions of his normal appetites as gifts of God and with praise and thanksgiving to the Giver and Creator. It is an essentially good creation. God called it into being. He spoke it into being with his creative Word. And God himself passed upon it the first and unalterable judgment: He saw that it was good.

Such is the faith of Israel, matured through the centuries and given classical expression in the priestly story of creation. It is a story which further defines and distills the faith of the community in affirming the true nature of the relationships fundamental to Israel's faith, the relationships of God and nature, God and man, and man and nature. As Israel knows no asceticism, so too she knows no pantheism: God is never equated with the universe or with the natural order. He is, to be sure, revealed in nature:

> The heavens are telling the glory of God

writes the psalmist (19:1); but in the next line the relationship is made clear:

> The firmament proclaims his handiwork.

All nature testifies to the glory of God; but Israel tends always to see God's primary and decisive self-revelation in the arena of history, not nature. Indeed, she comes to make the affirmation of God-as-Creator because of her prior conviction that God acts and reveals himself in history. If God is Lord of history, he must also be Lord of Creation, the Creator of the total environment of history.

The community of Israel knew in her history the fierce temptations of nature religion and later the fear of a fate decreed by heavenly bodies. She was surrounded by it for centuries, and its appeal and influence are clearly to be seen in her literature. But her rejection of it is nonetheless decisive and finds nowhere a more economical and penetrating formulation than that of Gen. 1. God called the natural order into being, and continues to sustain it. It is his creation. He stands outside of it, separate from it, its Creator, its Preserver, its Lord.

Israel's mature belief about the relationship of man and God is also here caught up and given succinct expression. Man is essentially a creature of God. This is the primary and most meaningful category of his existence—and it is a universal quality. Man—not Israelite man, but Man—is created being and, as such, owes his existence to the Creator.

> Know that the Lord is God!
> It is he that made us, and we are his. . . .
>
> [Ps. 100:3]

Man is and is not at one with the rest of creation. We could proceed more surely, here, if we could be certain of the meaning of the phrases "in our image" and "after our likeness" of Gen. 1:26. It is clear that early Israel conceived of God as having form and substance and it may be that these phrases reflect that early belief that man physically resembles the form of God. But there are many overtones in Israel's literature that justify other than physical implications. Suppose we look again at the 8th Psalm:

> Thou hast made him [man] little less than God,
> and dost crown him with glory and honor.

A more literal translation of the first line would read, "Thou didst make him lack little of God," and the sense of the statement is hardly to point up a physical resemblance. In the light of Israel's total faith and its expression in canonical literature, we can hardly be wrong in understanding the image and likeness of God in man as implying man's high potential in achievement and his inherent capacity for response to and communion with God.

Man's status as creature is unique in another way: he is given "dominion . . . over every living thing that moves upon the earth" (Gen. 1:28). Here again the story of creation gives expression to a quality of faith characteristic of the community of Israel. Although man is a creature of God whose physical destiny is ultimately dust (as with all other creatures), he is also at once the crown of creation, that created being to whose use all else in creation is committed by the creator:

Thou has given him dominion over the works of thy hands;
  thou has put all things under his feet.

[Ps. 8:6]

And this is cause for man's unceasing praise of the Creator;
the 8th Psalm begins and ends with the doxology:

O Lord, our Lord,
  how majestic is thy name in all the earth!

The story of creation in Gen. 1 moves finally to the most
characteristic institution in the outward expression of
Israel's faith—the Sabbath. The priestly perspective is nowhere more evident; yet the Sabbath is no less an affirmation
of a point of Israel's belief than, say, the God-man relationship. Israel's consistent and serious regard of her institutional
expressions of faith is attested early and late in her literature
and in writings of prophets, priests and historians. Here the
story gives the central institution—the Sabbath—its ultimate
projection, declaring that its authority is from the beginning, in the very pattern of divine creation. God himself
"rested on the seventh day from all his work which he had
done" (2:2).

This creation story is a deftly wrought, summary expression of much that was of primary significance in the matured
faith of Israel. We have said that Israel knew no asceticism,
nor any pantheism. We may add a third "ism"; for Israel
also knew no deism. We have said that Gen. 1 is Israel's
classical statement of her creation faith, but we have tried
to make it clear that its primary motivation is not at all an
objective interest in origins. In very fact, the creation faith
of Israel betrays neither here nor anywhere else in her
literature an interest in origins for the sake of origins. The
creation faith speaks from and back to historical human
existence. It is obviously not primarily or even significantly

concerned to say how, scientifically, descriptively, man came to be, but rather to define what man *is*, and what, in the creation faith, his existence *means*. The thrust of the story is not toward the past but directly to the ever-moving present. Israel's creation faith is a theological commentary on the meaning of existence.

This is a far cry from deism, which sees creation continuing in an orderly (or pure-chance) fashion on its own inherent power while the Creator takes an extended Sabbath rest, unmoved and immovable, unknown and unknowable. Israel's creation faith is dynamically and existentially conceived. It is a faith articulated, cherished and preserved because it distills some of the essence of Israel's understanding of God and man in the world and in history.

We who belong to a totally different community, in a later age, products of modern Western, not ancient Eastern modes of thought—we may agree that this is to speak of Gen. 1:1–2:4a in terms of the religious culture that produced the story. We may concede that this is what it said and meant to Israel; but *we* are reading the story now and in our perspective questions inevitably arise that could not in the nature of things have concerned Israel. We, and all of us in the West since the scientific revolution of the seventeenth century, have some exacting questions to put to the literature. If we understand what an Old Testament narrative means first in Israel's categories, we cannot escape the questions of our own categories. To be sure, we have been asking our own questions for a couple of hundred years now, more or less; but we have made no prior effort, nor indeed any effort at all, to understand and interpret the literature in terms of its internal meaning, its meaning within the community that produced it.

We are concerned, to a degree that Israel never was, with

matters of *fact*. We in the modern West, as compared with the ancient Israelite, have a highly developed analytical interest in all that confronts us. We are scientifically informed, and we apply consciously or unconsciously a scientific method of study. And so, in the story of creation before us, there are problems and questions which arise out of the difference between East and West and the gulf, measured in millennia, between that era and our own. We are struck by the story's now naïve, mythological representation of a universe structured much in the fashion of a three-story building: water and land of the flat earth are the first level (1:9), the firmament (heavens) the second (1:7), and above the firmament at a third level, more water (1:6, 7). As we are better and more accurate observers of our universe than they, so also we know infinitely more about the world's past than they. We have uncovered in modern times significant geological and biological information reaching back literally over hundreds of thousands of years; and in the light of this information we are compelled to reject quite categorically the assumption of Gen. 1 that this extended process and development occurred in six days.[3]

If it be argued, as some well-intentioned persons have, that we are to read the word "day" as representing tens of thousands of years, we would have to ask, "What for, and on what grounds?" Is it to rationalize the story, to bring the story into conformity with a scientific view of natural and human development? And if for the sake of argument we concede that this is a possible reading of the word "day" (which in fact it is not) what then? How shall we also rationalize the three-story universe, which is assumed everywhere in the entire Bible in one form or another? And how, if this is the sense of day, are we to interpret one obvious and climactic motive of the story—the establishment of the ultimate authority of the Sabbath institution? The Hebrew word for "day" is *yōm*, used with great regularity in the literature of Israel for the unit of time from sundown to sundown, or for the period of light as distinguished from the period of darkness. It may refer to a more extensive unit of time in the past and especially the future, but never with the abstraction and comprehensiveness implicit in our term "eon."[4]

Efforts to rationalize, then, can be and often are self-defeating, that is, they may obscure the first aim of Old Testament study—the understanding of what Israel thought and believed. The more we erroneously impute our own modern categories to Israel, the less are we able to recover the faith of Israel. If Israel believed, with scientific inaccuracy to be sure, that the created universe came into being in six days, the expression of this view informs us of the quality of her faith. Israel nowhere views the natural order as we do —and we must understand this before we can understand Israel.

Our own necessarily critical approach is never, then, ultimately negative in purpose and result; it often enables us to see and understand something of peculiar significance in the life of Israel which we might otherwise miss altogether. For example, we observe that the creation of light (1:3), the separation of day and night (1:4 f.), the phenomenon of evening and morning (vv. 5, 8, 13), and the appearance of vegetation (1:11 f.) all precede the making of the "two great lights" (sun and moon, 1:16). We know that light comes from the sun, that darkness is the absence of light, and that the growth of vegetation requires the sun's rays. But a little reflection will inform us that Israel must have known this too—the knowledge is partially reflected in vv. 16-18. This is not, then, like the three-story universe, a prescientific discrepancy. Rather, this seeming contradiction of Israel's own observation of natural phenomena emphasizes her insistence that God is more than a nature deity, and that natural laws are subject to his will. The contradiction further suggests a characteristic quality in Israel's writings —her relative indifference to concerns of logical consistency. In the recording, editing and compiling of her literature, Israel is simply not disturbed, as we inevitably are, by matters of logical contradiction.

Finally, our critical, analytical reading of the story raises a further problem: we cannot but note the inclusion of two different modes of creation. If God creates by divine Word ("God said, Let there be . . ."), he also creates by Work (God made, or created, vv. 7, 16, 21, 25, 27). Apparently a concept of creation by work has at some point along the way in Israel's tradition had superimposed upon it a more spiritualized concept of creation by word. If so, Israel characteristically retains both modes and sees no necessary incompatibility: the created universe is God's, who not only called it into being, but labored to produce it.

B. Of Dust from the Ground (Gen. 2:4b–3:24)

Other questions arise as soon as we continue our reading of chapter 2. V. 4a, "These are the generations of . . . ," is a kind of signature. It occurs ten times in the book of Genesis, with one or two minor variations (2:4, 5:1, 6:9, 10:1, 11:10, 11:27, 25:12, 25:19, 36:1[9], and 37:2) and always in a sharply transitional context. It is a characteristic term of the Priestly writers and is here obviously employed as the conclusion of the story of creation begun in Gen. 1:1.

Unmistakably, a second distinct story of creation begins in the middle of 2:4. The verse division here and in many other places is unsatisfactory and inappropriate; but it is well to remember that current verse division was first introduced relatively late, not, in fact, until the tenth century of our era. Scholars have through the years expressed their disaffection with the present versification in repeating the perennial story that verse divisions were first entered in the text by a man riding on horseback.

The first conspicuous difference between the two stories is in vocabulary. The P (priestly) account of creation (Gen. 1:1–2:4a) consistently uses the term "God" from the Hebrew *elohim*. But in Gen. 2-3 it is characteristically a double term *YHWH elohim*, translated in the King James and Revised Standard Versions, "the LORD God" but in the American Revised Version, "Jehovah God." Jehovah was dropped in the recent American revision (the R.S.V.) because of its unsatisfactory nature as a hybrid word. The Hebrew language was written without vowels until a system of supplying vowels to the consonants was evolved over a period of several centuries early in our era by a continuing group of devoted scholars known as the Masoretes. They received a sacred tradition which forbade the articulation of the divine name, written with the four consonants, YHWH, a tradition which supplied, wherever the divine name appeared, the word *adonai*, meaning "Lord." Understandably, the Masoretes sought to continue the tradition by supplying the vowels of *"adonai"* to the consonantal root YHWH, giving rise to the hybrid word Jehovah. While we do not know and probably never can recover with certainty the original pronunciation of the name of Israel's deity, our best guess is "Yahweh."

The recognition of two creation stories in Genesis was the primary item in the beginnings of modern biblical criticism, a recognition first made in 1680 by a French priest named Simon. In 1753 another Frenchman, Astruc, a physician by profession, pointed out the use of divine names as the chief distinguishing mark of the two stories; and a little later, in

1780, the German scholar Eichhorn recorded other differences in vocabulary between the two creation accounts. The letter Y in YHWH, representing the Hebrew letter *yodh*, was transliterated J; and J (for JHWH) became the symbol to designate not only the second creation story but in time a considerable body of texts in the Hexateuch (Genesis-Joshua) showing some of the same peculiarities of vocabulary, style and point of view.

We note that differences in vocabulary are not confined to the divine name. P (Gen. 1–2:4a) uses the verbs "create" and "make" while J (Gen. 2:4b ff.) uses "form" (literally, "to model") and, of woman, a verb literally meaning "to build." Where P speaks of beasts "of the earth" it is "of the field" in J.

But differences in vocabulary are less conspicuous than fundamental differences in representation:

	P	J
Earth's original state	A watery chaos	A waterless waste
Time span	Six days	No time reference
Order of Creation	1. Light	Man, out of dust
	2. Firmament	The Garden
	3. Land, by separation from water	Trees, including *the* tree (see below)
	4. Vegetation	Animals, beasts and birds (fish not mentioned)
	5. Heavenly bodies	Woman, out of man
	6. Birds and fishes	
	7. Animals and man, both sexes	

The orderliness, the dignity, the repetitive phrasing, the obvious purposiveness (absolute authority of the Sabbath), and the relative sophistication of the P account[5] are replaced in J with a charming and intimate naïveté. In vocabulary, in content and in total concept, the two stories appear to be so different that we cannot but wonder how and why both came to be included in this introduction to the literature of Israel.

We must look for the answer first in the postexilic (fifth century B.C.) theocratic community which brought the Pentateuch (Gen.–Deut.) together in its present form. Clearly, in this matured perspective of Israel's faith and history, the corporate editorial mind endorses and retains on behalf of the community both stories of creation because, despite their differences (and perhaps *in* their very divergence), only the two stories in combination give adequate expression to Israel's creation faith, to her interpretation of the essential nature of man as a creature of God. We have good reason to think that the second story of creation came into literary currency in Israel as early, probably, as the tenth century B.C. (perhaps in a somewhat shorter form than now); that it was then incorporated into a continuous narrative still discernible as the primary literary structure upon which our present Hexateuch (Gen.–Josh.) is built; that the editor, whom we call the Yahwist, composed his document (J) in the main from individual stories and cycles of stories (oral and [?] written) of earlier and widely diversified origin; and that he achieved, largely by means of selection and arrangement (not revision) of these materials a remarkably unified and theologically coherent work.

From where we stand, we recognize, then, that we have to deal with three different levels of interpretation. The first and earliest level is that of the story's primitive origin, before the Yahwist employed it for his own purposes in the J opus. We suspect that at this level the primary motivation of the creation stories and most of the material in Gen. 1-11 is an etiological motivation, that is, a prescientific, mythological effort to explain persistent and common questions of origin as, for example, of the world (1), of the relationship of man and woman (2:18 ff.), of the nature of sex (3:6 ff.), of pain in childbirth (3:16), of the necessity of human labor (3:17 ff.), or, again, the origin of music (4:21), or of men of unusually great stature (6:1 ff.), or of wine and its effects (9:20 f.), or of the dispersion of peoples and the variety of languages in the world (11:1 ff.).

But while we can be reasonably certain that these stories came into being at the first level under an etiological motive, and while the motivation leaves its clear mark on the stories as we read them now, we can be equally sure that this was by no means their primary significance at the second level, the level of their incorporation in the epic work of the Yahwist, or the third level, that of the final editorial work of the postexilic community.

The Yahwist constructs his work around the central theme of divine promise and fulfillment: the promise is made to Abraham in Gen. 12:1 ff. (and subsequently repeated to Isaac and Jacob) that (1) Abraham's descendants shall become a great people and (2) they shall be given a homeland; and the promise is fulfilled in the formation of the people under Moses and the conquest of Palestine under Joshua. But that the Yahwist himself understands God's concern and activity on Israel's behalf as having ultimate implications beyond this is unmistakably indicated in a third promise, not fulfilled in the scope of the Yahwist's work: in Abraham all the nations of the earth will be blessed. He prefaces his work with much of what is now contained in Gen. 2-11 certainly not as an etiological but as a theological prelude—a prelude setting forth the fundamental terms of God's relationship to man in the world, a prelude justifying and explaining

the peculiarity of God's particular activity on behalf of
Israel.

With the third level of interpretation, we return to the
postexilic community from whose perspective the whole of
Israel's history is surveyed. The unexplicit and ultimately
inexplicable conviction of the Yahwist that the promise to
Abraham embraces a function infinitely beyond mere state-
hood has been further articulated by the prophets in their
eloquent and inspired interpretation of Israel's hectic history
from the tenth to the fifth centuries, and most pointedly in
the words of a prophet who interprets the meaning of exile
and restoration:

> It is too light a thing that you [Israel] should be my servant
>   to raise up the tribes of Jacob
>   and to restore the preserved of Israel;
> I will give you as a light to the nations,
>   that my salvation may reach to the end of the earth.
>
> [Isa. 49:6]

How and why, then, do both creation stories come to be
included in this introduction, this prelude, to the literature
of Israel? What the Yahwist *essentially* intended to com-
municate in his story of creation in the tenth century is endorsed and confirmed in the fifth. At both levels the story
serves a theological, not an etiological, purpose: it reflects
the faith of Israel, early and late, about the meaning of existence. The later community, the mature community, simply
underlines, in the addition of the first story, the absolutely
universal purpose of God in his choice of Israel and his activity in her own and the wider environment of history.
Israel ultimately must include both stories because, as we
have already suggested, only the two together return a full

expression—we could as well use the word "confession"—of her faith. The stories are complementary.

And this is to read the stories with empathy, from within the community. Creation is good. Divinely surveyed in its completed totality, it is "very good" (1:31). God is graciously disposed to man: his is a beneficent will (1:28 f.). All of this, in divine intention, is universal. In more intimate, in more highly personalized terms, this is reaffirmed in the second, older story, the J account. Yet the beneficent will of God is more. God labors in man's creation (2:7). He himself plants the garden, man's rich and pleasing environment (2:8). Seeing his creature's loneliness he makes him—almost—a partner in creation: every living creature is brought into being and presented for approval, and a *name*. And for Israel, to give the name is to share responsibly in the very being of that which is named. Israel would never concur in our dictum that a rose by any other name would smell as sweet; because for Israel a rose by some other name could not be a rose: the name is of the very essence of that which is named. The entire passage, 2:18-22, understands man as the object of God's love—nothing less—and a partner, almost, in creation. This suggests the possibility of an even warmer quality in the psalmist's line,

> Thou hast made man little less than God. . . .

But love must give freedom, and freedom requires the will to choose and an understanding of alternative choices. It is, to be sure, a good creation, and an altogether good and loving Creator—but Israel knows not only in her neighbors but in herself the freedom of will to choose not the good but the evil. Consistently, Israel looks realistically at human initiative, an initiative symbolized in the creation story in "the tree."

The second story (J), like the first (P), shows signs that it came to its present form in a long process; and nowhere does it show its composite nature more clearly than in the various ways in which "the tree" is designated. In the unit, Gen. 2-3, the forbidden tree is referred to as:

1. the tree of life, 2:9, 3:22
2. the tree of the knowledge of good and evil, 2:9, 17 (and cf 3:5, 22)
3. the tree that is simply prohibited, without further definition, 3:11, 17
4. the tree in the midst of the garden, 2:9, 3:3

From where we stand, it appears probable that the present story (Gen. 2:4b ff.) of the Garden-Creation preserves two originally independent accounts. One sought in some way to deal with the vexing question of human mortality (the tree of life) and the other, at a primitive level, with the equally perplexing problem of evil. Both accounts were clearly etiological, that is, both represent an effort to explain existing phenomena in terms of origins; and both themes appear to have been borrowed outside Israel.

But the very confusion in terms in the present story strongly suggests that within the Israelite community the story is shaped and preserved by faith, that Israel is concerned not so significantly with the intrinsic properties of the tree as with what the tree represents, what it symbolizes. Israel's stress is on the third and fourth designations above. The forbidden tree represents the essential difference between Creator and man; it defines the central requisite for their harmonious relationship—obedience; and it leaves no doubt that obedience requires faith, that on any other terms than faith (e.g., human reason) man will rebel rather than obey:

So when the woman saw that the tree was good for food, and that it was a delight to the eyes, and that the tree was to be desired to make one wise, she took of its fruit and ate; and she also gave some to her husband, and he ate.

[3:6]

The forbidden tree represents the authority of the Creator over man; but it also represents his love. The forbidden tree is alone the symbol of man's freedom of will, his freedom of choice. Man-in-the-image-of-God can be no automaton. He possesses *will:* he is a *responsible* being.

Israel puts its emphasis upon the symbol of forbiddenness; but also, with an imprecision inherent in the character of the story, upon the location of the tree "in the midst of the garden." It is Israel's intuitive articulation of faith that the decision of human will is never peripheral but "in the midst," that the choice of obedience or rebellion is always in the center, always the central quality of human life in creation.

So it is that the unit, Gen. 2-3, moves on to give a theological explanation, universally applicable, of why the good creation, the beneficent divine will, the love of God, and the harmonious relationship between God and man, all appear to be distorted, fragmented and broken. We recall the words of Thomas Mann about the meaning of myth, the truth of myth: "It is, it always is, however much we may say, it was." Certainly this expresses Israel's understanding of these stories. These are stories, not about what *was*, but what *is*. This is Israel's commentary on the nature of existence. Human existence is in broken and distorted relationship with God and creation because man is not obedient. Man rebels against his status as creature, he rejects the limitation set upon his creatureliness (symbolized in the forbidden tree), he repudiates faith in the Creator in favor of his own powers —and God must act against him in judgment.

The two stories are complementary. The frustrations and tragedies of human existence—expulsion from the Garden —are the unhappy outcome of a good creation by a good God (Gen. 1) because man exercises his power of will, his responsibility, his great gift of likeness to God, in prideful rebellion against his Creator and Sustainer. The full faith, the rounder understanding, is conveyed in neither story alone, but only in both. The one account in this respect is essentially summarized in the words, "God created man in his own image"; the other, in the words, "God formed man of dust from the ground." Neither alone is an adequate expression of Israel's faith. Together, they define what Israel believes about man—his high potential in the purpose and love of God, and at the same time his sinful, rebellious performance: in the image of God, of dust from the ground.

C. Out to the Field (Gen. 4:1-16)

We have seen two stories of creation, one early (2:4b ff.) and the other relatively late (1:1 ff.). We acknowledge the differences between the two, and we attempt to classify and define the differences in terms of larger and at one time independently integrated sources—J and P respectively. Both stories are shaped by the continuing community of Israel. Both result from and give expression to the faith of Israel, a faith which was itself created and formed and sustained in a very real history of very real events from the Exodus to the Monarchy to the Exile and into the Restoration of Israel. The two stories are endorsed by the mature community and testify not only to certain differences in perspective in the long course of Israel's history but also and significantly to the perpetuity, the consistency and the essential unity of Israel's faith.

In Gen. 3 we have surveyed an account inseparably integrated with the J account of creation immediately preceding, an account whose *raison d'être* in Israel's sacred literature lies in its explanation, in theological terms, of the universal human plight. Human life is fraught with tension, labor, pain and frustration because of human sin—pride, rebellion, disobedience—and divine judgment against it. And the three major narratives which follow also revolve, like that of the Garden, around the central theme of sin and judgment. This is the primary theme of the stories of the Garden (Gen. 3), of Cain and Abel (Gen. 4), of the Flood (Gen. 6-9) and of the Tower of Babel (Gen. 11). Each deals with a different aspect of man's prideful rebellion against his Creator and Sustainer, issuing in alienation not only of man from God, but man from man as well.

In each of the four stories, then, it is implicitly an act of rebellion against God which provokes the divine judgment; but each story sees the act in a different expression. In the first story, the sin, the rebellion, takes the form of disobedience:

She took of its fruit [the forbidden tree] and ate; and she also gave some to her husband, and he ate.

[3:6b]

In the second, it is wanton violence within the human community:

And when they were in the field, Cain rose up against his brother Abel, and killed him.

[4:8b]

In the third, the story of the Flood, the sin of rebellion is yet more flagrant: the perversion of human will against divine will takes the form of moral depravity:

Yahweh saw that the wickedness of man was great in the earth, and that every imagination of the thoughts of his heart was only evil continually.

[6:5]

And in the fourth, the account of Babel, rebellion is total and overt. It is rejection of God. It is apostasy, the repudiation of God, the abandonment of faith:

Then they [men] said, "Come, let *us* build *ourselves* a city, and a tower with its top in the heavens, and let *us* make a *name* for *ourselves*, lest we be scattered abroad upon the face of the whole earth."

[11:4]

Israel sees the divine judgment in each of the four expressions of rebellion as peculiarly appropriate to the human act. Disobedience of God issues in alienation and separation of God and man; human violence, in alienation and separation of man from man; moral depravity, in destruction and death; and apostasy, the denial of faith, the assertion of self-sufficiency, in wholesale human division, discord and misunderstanding.

We inject this brief survey of what immediately precedes and follows the story under discussion (Cain and Abel) because the interpretation of any biblical text is dependent ultimately upon its *context*. In Genesis in particular, stories representing a wide variety of origins and unquestionably transmitted at one time independently of one another have been put together with relatively little alteration in the form in which they were received. Their meaning to Israel, their function as an articulation of the faith of Israel, lies primarily in the process of selection and arrangement and integration. If we are to understand Gen. 4 we must see it in its purposeful relationship to its wider contexts, that is,

to (1) Gen. 3-11, (2) Gen. 1-11 (3) Gen. 1-50, (4) the canon of
Israel, the Old Testament and (5) for the Christian, the
entire Bible.

And with respect to these relationships, it is important to
remark again that the stories of Gen. 1-11 are together a
theological commentary on Israel's view of the universal
relationship between God and man. The four primary literary units in Gen. 3-11 constitute a *universal* indictment
of what *is,* not an antiquarian "historical" commentary on
what *was.* The indictment, then, of Gen. 3, and of the section
Gen. 3-11, is universal—and Israel herself is *not* an exception. Israel's historians, prophets and writers in the main
insist that Israel too stands under the same indictment with
all men. Israel understands the meaning of her own history
in part in terms of sin and judgment.

The primeval history in Gen. 1-11 is in its essential structure and unity the work of J (the Yahwist); but it was received, endorsed and at points expanded by P. At both levels,
Israel sees her own peculiar function and mission, pointedly
introduced with the call of Abraham in Gen. 12, against the
background of an ever-widening gulf between God and man,
and between man and man. This is Israel's faith. Man's sin
of rebellion against God—whether in the form of disobedience, violence, depravity or apostasy—is always divinely
judged and punished.

But it is important to observe that divine judgment,
severe as it is, is never without the quality of divine mercy.
Man is expelled from the Garden, but his life continues with
every indication of divine concern. Cain is expelled from
his own community, yet he is granted divine protection.
Man is destroyed, but not quite: the destruction is sub-
servient to the divine mercy which seeks to give opportunity
for a new beginning. Man is dispersed and divided by funda-

mental misunderstandings, but again life is continued in the divine hope that man will come to know the one source of unity and peace. The divine judgment is never merely punitive in character: it is ultimately redemptive in purpose.

If this is the theological sense of the primeval history, and if, in particular, the Cain-Abel story illustrates the common sin of violence and its consequences; if this is the appropriate interpretation at the levels of J and P, we, nevertheless, cannot escape questions which arise out of indications of other motives, other concerns, which are still latent in the story.

We suspect at once that the story originally had no connection with the account of the expulsion from the Garden in Gen. 3. The two accounts appear to have been somewhat artificially joined in 4:1-2a; and we note in addition several presuppositions of the Cain-Abel plot which suggest that the story originally had a different setting:

1. the existence of a clan or tribe to take revenge on Cain
2. the existence of another clan or tribe in which Cain finds refuge, and a wife
3. the existence of the religious institution of sacrifice which in turn presupposes a rather highly developed religious organization.

We have already noted Israel's indifference to matters of logical conformity; and we suspect that what appears as a discrepancy to us results in fact from singleness of editorial purpose—not chronological sequence, but theological commentary.

If we ask the question—and we can hardly escape it— What was the function of the story at levels prior to its incorporation in the primeval story? more than one possibility is suggested. The story breathes a tribal atmosphere:

did it originate and was it pridefully preserved first among tribesmen who counted their descent from Cain, who regarded him as their ancestor? Is this a story which comes to Israel from the Cainites, who become Kenites and who are subsequently seen in the Old Testament as related to, and associated with, the Israelites?

Or does the story reflect the ancient memory, a common memory among seminomadic tribes, of antipathy between the agriculturalist (Cain) and the nomad (Abel)? Was this its original primary function?

Or could the story come to us from the original form of what is known as a cult myth? According to this view, the story is the verbal deposit of an ancient fertility ritual: it describes a primitive cultic function, a kind of sacrifice, performed to assure a rich yield to the field. Cain is the priestly person, and Abel the sacrificial victim whose blood, shed upon the ground, will bring necessarily the response of fertility. The flight of Cain is a ritual flight: he is defiled by his act and must purify himself in flight. At the same time, he is acting on behalf of the community, whose protecting mark is put upon him.[6]

Any of these explanations, alone or in combination, is a possible interpretation of the story at a preliterary level. It is not impossible that the story sustained even in early times an interpretation placing heavy emphasis on v. 9:

Then the Lord said to Cain, "Where is Abel your brother?" He said, "I do not know; am I my brother's keeper?"

In view of the wealth of legal and prophetic material in the Old Testament reflecting the sense of corporate responsibility, we are certain that this element of the story had profound meaning for Israel. It is indeed inseparably related to the primary theological theme and purpose of the story in its present context. True community is realized only under God, in conformity to the righteous will of God. Violation of the divine terms for community results in divine judgment—disruption of community and separation from God. In context, the story gives expression to Israel's theological explanation of the brokenness of all community everywhere: it is precisely man's denial that he is his brother's keeper; and the denial is itself an act of rebellion against God.

And the Lord said, ". . . The voice of your brother's blood is crying to me from the ground." . . . Cain said to the Lord, ". . . thou hast driven me this day away from the ground; and from thy face I shall be hidden; and I shall be a fugitive and a wanderer on the earth. . . ."

[4:10, 13 f., in part]

D. When Men Began to Multiply (Gen. 6-9)

The first four verses of chapter 6 appear to have had no original connection with the story of the Flood. They are placed here, probably by the Yahwist, because in the editor's interpretation the incident points to the sinfulness of men and it contributes, therefore, to his theme of the increasing moral depravity of the world. We note the probable etiological motive that first gave rise to the story. The occasional phenomenon of men of unusually great stature—in our own circuses they are called giants—led to the belief, widely held in antiquity, of the existence of a lost race of giants. The opening verses of chapter 6 explain the belief as the result of a union between the "sons of God" and the "daughters of men."

The story of the Flood no doubt preserves an ancient historical recollection of severe inundation; but it is, we think, no longer necessary to enumerate all of the reasons why this account centering in the person of Noah cannot be regarded as factual.[7] Israel in her historical existence in Canaan never knew a serious threat from flood. The story is borrowed, apparently from Babylonia, not for what it says about water, land, animals and ark, but for what it says about the relationship of God and man.

It is borrowed from Babylonia, where severe floods were known and are archaeologically attested, in two forms apparently (possibly three)—one taken over by J and the other by P. While the accounts are now interwoven, it is not difficult to separate the most important features of each.[8]

J	*P*
Seven pairs of clean animals, and one pair of unclean animals (a distinction reflecting dietary laws) are taken into the ark, 7:2 f.	Two of all animals, male and female, 6:19 f., 7:15 f.
The Flood is caused by rain,	The fountains of the great deep below, and the windows of heaven above, are opened, reflecting the concept of a three- or possibly a four-storied universe, 7:11.
The Flood lasts for forty days, 7:12 (cf. 7:17), and subsides after two (or three?) periods of seven days, 8:6 ff.	The Flood remains for 150 days, 7:24, and is ended, apparently, in 150 days, 8:3.
The sending forth of raven and dove, 8:6 ff.	
Noah offers a sacrifice, 8:20.	The ark finally comes aground on the mountains of Ararat, 8:4.
Yahweh (R.S.V.: the Lord) smells its pleasing odor, 8:21.	

Yahweh declares that he will never again thus curse the ground; and he adds, in effect, that he must find other means to solve the problem of human perverseness—"for the imagination of man's heart is evil from his youth." 8:21.

God makes a covenant with Noah, to which covenant the rainbow remains the permanent testimony: "never again shall there be a flood to destroy the earth." 9:8 ff.

We note again one of the chief distinguishing characteristics of J and P: J uses the term Yahweh for the divine name, while P, as in Gen. 1, prefers the more general designation God, in Hebrew, *elohim*. This is a consistent feature of the priestly stratum in Genesis, conforming to the view that the name Yahweh was first revealed to Moses, and through him, to Israel (see Ex. 6:2 ff.).

If the modern reader finds these internal contradictions and discrepancies a little disconcerting, it is all the more important to observe what is stressed in the story without any ambiguity. The Flood marks the end of one epoch and the beginning of another. Man and the world are given a fresh start, a new and clean beginning. Chapter 9:1 ff. (P) makes of it a restitution of the original terms of creation and adds significant ritual and moral requirements:

Be fruitful and multiply, and fill the earth. . . . Every moving thing that lives shall be food for you; . . . I give you everything. Only you shall not eat flesh with its life, that is, its blood [the requirement that the blood, the life principle, is God's, and may not be eaten]. . . . of every man's brother I will require the life of man. . . . for God made man in his own image.

J also understands a restored creation:

While the earth remains, seedtime and harvest, cold and heat, summer and winter, day and night, shall not cease.

[8:22]

Similarly, although P alone uses the actual term "covenant," both strands of the narrative agree in a profoundly significant confession of faith, which is so articulated in the combination of the two together that one suspects not only "method in the madness" that united them, but also sheer inspiration.[9] If we accept the story as finally Israel did in its present unity, we are given deep insight into her faith. God acts in severe judgment upon the perversity, the moral depravity of man. If the character of God is thus apparently portrayed in harsh terms, it is surely intended to underline not any inadequacy in God, but the incredible depth of human ingratitude which in wholesale fashion defies the love that brought man into being and prostitutes a capacity and nature divinely conceived precisely for harmonious community with man and God. In the Flood story, Israel expresses her faith not in an unmerciful God, but in a God of grace.

It is the sense of the story that the life of man *deserves* extinction. The anthropomorphic terms—*God* in the image of *man*—are retained in Israel long after the primitive concepts which shaped the original language are transcended.

And the Lord was sorry that he had made man on the earth, and it grieved him to his heart. So the Lord said, "I will blot out man whom I have created from the face of the ground, man and beast and creeping things and birds of the air, for I am sorry that I made them."

[6:6 f.]

At an early level of the story, this is certainly to be interpreted as reflecting the notion of a highly limited deity who, like man, makes his mistakes and lives to regret them, to acknowledge them, and to attempt to rectify them. But in the full context of Israel's mature faith, we understand that she retains the old language with a different interpretation. How, more pointedly and economically, can Israel give expression to her own view that man in his desecration of creation deserves to be wiped out?

Yet God's very judgment is given in love and compassion and mercy! The life of man is not extinguished but is instead given a new beginning, a fresh start. The old slate is wiped clean. That this renewal of life is something that always *is*—not simply *was*—is expressed in the designation of the rainbow as the perpetual sign of God's mercy. It is the sign of God's commitment in solemn covenant to the whole of creation in perpetuity, despite the fact that (8:21) "the imagination of man's heart" remains continually evil:

Then God said to Noah and to his sons with him, "Behold, I establish my covenant with you and your descendants after you [i.e., all men, in all time]. . . . I set my bow in the cloud, and it shall be a sign of the covenant between me and the earth. . . . When the bow is in the clouds, I will look upon it and remember the everlasting covenant between God and every living creature of all flesh that is upon the earth."

[9:8, 13, 16]

It is the faith of Israel that God is Creator, Sustainer and Judge, that he reveals himself in nature and in history, and that he is committed to *all* human life in love and mercy and profound concern. We cannot rightly understand Israel's view of her own peculiar divine election and covenant except against this background of her faith in God's covenant with all men, in all time.

E. ITS NAME WAS CALLED BABEL (GEN. 11:1-9)

The etiological motive, the primitive effort to explain existing phenomena in terms of origin, is a marked feature of the story of the building of the city and the tower. We suspect that the account in its present form combines two distinct etiologies:

> Then they said, "Come, let us build ourselves a city, and a tower with its top in the heavens, and let us make a name for ourselves, lest we be scattered abroad upon the face of the earth."
>
> [Gen. 11:4]

One etiology may originally have been created to explain the actual ruins of an ancient tower. According to this story, the builders constructed the tower in order to establish a name for themselves and they are divinely judged with the confusion of their speech, vv. 7, 9a. At an early level the story served the further etiological function of explaining the multiplicity of human languages. The other etiology has its beginning in a city, not a tower, a city built to insure the unity and security of its builders. The judgment is dispersion, vv. 8, 9b, explaining etiologically the wide geographic distribution of peoples.

The two narratives, if originally distinct, are now skillfully combined. Other than the duplicates noted, which are in any case in remarkable affinity, the story is inconsistent in only one particular—the two references to Yahweh's coming down in vv. 5 and 7. It retains the naïveté of its early origin in representing all mankind as a single nomadic group with "one language and few words" and in explaining with charming economy the transition in language and location from simple unity to complex diversity.

In the context of what precedes and follows the story of Babel, we understand that Israel preserves this brief narrative for its contribution to the expression of her faith. Like the stories of the Garden, of Cain and of the Flood, Babel illustrates a central quality of human sin, and the nature of divine judgment. If at an early level the story (or its two separate strands) was taken to focus on what *was*, Israel clearly reads it as a commentary on what also *is*. Man presumes to effect his own security: he puts his ultimate trust in himself and in his own efforts, as if God did not exist. The judgment, under which all men live and from which all men suffer, is division, misunderstanding and antagonism. The theological essence of the story is an absolutely uncompromising faith: the multiple and tragic divisions within the human family result from pride and arrogance, self-trust and self-worship; the resolution, by unmistakable implication, lies only in acceptance of the status of creature, in faith in God.

Suppose we paraphrase the story in terms of our own times in an effort to translate the uncompromising nature of Israel's faith:

And as men journeyed through history, they came to the valley of the shadow of destruction and settled there. And they said to one another, "Come, let us make that which will cause wars to cease." And they had the dread of Hiroshima for brick, and for mortar the fear of weapons yet more terrible. They then said, "Come, let us build ourselves one kingdom of men, which shall be our salvation. And let us make a name for ourselves throughout all the ages, lest, indeed, we destroy ourselves upon the face of the whole earth.

And the Lord, uninvoked, came down to see all the efforts of the children of men to save the world by the means of the children of men. And the Lord said, "Behold, they would be one people, and they would have all one language. But I am their unity, and they have not called upon my name. Their common language is in me, and they know me not. Therefore, the kingdom of men is confounded, and its name shall be called Babel until the children of men are united in me, by my spirit."

In one significant respect, the story of Babel differs from the three major narrative units that precede it in the primeval history. The four stories together all declare that human life is derelict because man rebels against God. Human life is unfulfilled and unfulfilling because it is lived under judgment and in a state of alienation of man from God and man from man. It may well be that the stories are arranged so as to convey a progressive broadening of the chasm between God and man. And yet the first three stories understand a corresponding act of divine grace, of divine mercy, of divine concern. Man is expelled from the Garden; but God himself clothes his creatures, human life continues and God acts not in a justice which would decree death, but in mercy fraught with hope. Cain is expelled from the community; yet he continues under divine protection and lives to establish a new community (4:17 ff.). The Flood destroys, to be sure, but not utterly: if the judgment is severe, the divine grace is correspondingly powerfully expressed; for man is in mercy given a new start, a new beginning fraught again with hope.

In all of these God's forgiveness is implicit, his sustaining power is explicit and above all his concern to bring about a reconciliation of himself and man is pointed and emphatic. Why is this positive note so conspicuously missing in the story of Babel? Life is permitted to continue, to be sure, but under what appears to be the unremitting, unrelieved and unqualified judgment of the fragmentation of mankind in widespread dispersion and in multiple mutual misunderstanding and alienation. Judgment *appears* to be the final divine word.

The story of Babel is the climax of the primeval history. If, as we have suggested, the faith of Israel is portrayed primarily in the selection and arrangement of the stories, and if Gen. 3-11 is constructed in such a way as to convey a progressive estrangement between man and God, this story illustrates the ultimate act of rebellion—the total denial of God in the absolute assumption of self-sufficiency. This is sin in totality, with finality. It is rebellion in greater intensity and degree than disobedience, or violence, or even moral depravity. The judgment is appropriate: the punishment fits the crime.

And yet, it is precisely here that the story of man's estrangement from God is inseparably joined to the great biblical theme of God's initiating, active concern to bridge the chasm. It is precisely here that the tragedies and frustrations of alienation are resolved in the anticipation of divine purpose, love and promise. Babel is *not* the final word of the primeval history. The theological conclusion of the section, Gen. 1-11, is in the first verses of Gen. 12. The call of Abraham, and particularly the divine promise of Gen. 12:3, is at once the conclusion of the primeval history and the beginning of the story of God's reconciling and redeeming activity. From the welter of peoples and tongues, Abraham is called for one express and ultimate purpose: ". . . in you all the families of the earth will be blessed."[10]

This is the faith of Israel. This is essentially what Israel believes about man and about God. It is in the light of this faith that she understands herself.

F. These are the Generations

These are the major components of the primeval history. We will look briefly now at the remaining passages in Gen. 1-11. In Gen. 5 we have an extended and detailed genealogy obviously from the same priestly stratum responsible for Gen. 1 (note especially the vocabulary and phrasing of vv. 1 and 2). These are given—we are sure, naïvely—as the generations from Adam to the sons of Noah. Such a table as this reflects the view, held in common by the Israelites and other ancient peoples, that in very early times men had enjoyed a much longer life span. If these figures on longevity seem extreme, we may recall a parallel list of ten Babylonian kings preceding the Flood who together reigned for a remarkable total of 432,000 years![11]

In contrast to P's clerical, repetitive table of generations, J (Gen. 4:17-26) records the line of human succession—a list which closely corresponds—with three marked differences. The J genealogy is a much more colorful piece of writing, often retaining with the name an item of interesting etiological data. Cain originates the building of cities; Jabal, "the father of those who dwell in tents and have cattle," is the first nomad; his brother Jubal apparently is the originator of music as "the father of all those who play the lyre and pipe"; Tubal-cain is the first smith, "the forger of all instruments of bronze and iron"; Lamech is the originator of the principle of blood revenge, in a poem, incidentally, of extreme antiquity (vv. 23, 24); and it is Enosh, or men in his time, who first call upon the name of Yahweh. This introduces a second point of difference between the genealogies of J and P: as we have already noted, the P stratum records in Exod. 6:3 ff. the contradicting view that men first call upon the name of Yahweh in the time of Moses. A third striking difference is that this piece is drawn from a source which either reflects ignorance of the Flood, or has been editorially curtailed somewhere along the way.

This is not, of course, to say that the Yahwist, the J source as a whole, is ignorant of the Flood, since one of the two

major strands of the present Flood story is from J. And at
the conclusion of the Flood account, Gen. 9:18-28, we have
an enigmatic little piece, much like Gen. 4:17 ff., about
Noah and his sons. This, too, has the same naïve and etiological atmosphere of the earlier J genealogy. Ham is the
progenitor of the Canaanites; Noah is the first agriculturalist, and the founder of the first distillery, to his own embar-
rassment; which episode sets the scene for another matter of
etiological information, the explanation in terms of origin
of the subjugation of Canaan (Ham) to the descendants of
Japheth and particularly Shem, the father of all Semites,
and consequently of the tribes of Israel.

The full genealogy of Shem is given in 11:10 ff. in the
characteristic style of P. It traces the descendants of Shem
to Abraham who, as we shall see, is seen in Genesis as the
progenitor not only of Israel, but of many nations and
peoples.

In Chapter 10 we have another genealogy, "the generations of the sons of Noah, Shem, Ham, and Japheth." It is
clear that J and P are combined here, whatever the nature of
the original sources from which the material is drawn. The
etiological quality of the J genealogy appears especially in
the section from v. 8 to v. 19, in v. 21, and again in vv. 25-30.
And again we are struck with the logical inconsistency of
the literature: here, in contradiction to the story of Babel,
the geographical distribution of peoples is understood as
the result of a long process of expansion, migration and
settlement. It is not, of course, a strictly accurate, scientific
ethnology. We could hardly expect this. But it does represent a more rational effort to explain the phenomenon of
race and language and the dispersion of peoples.

The major components of Gen. 1-11 are drawn from
ancient, non-Israelite mythologies. They are selected, edited

and arranged as a universal theological commentary whose primary quality is not was-ness but is-ness. God *is* Creator-Sustainer, Judge, and—always implicitly—Reconciler. Man *is* a rebellious creature in his disobedience, violence, wickedness and self-deification. This remains the divine-human tension in which Israel's historical role is understood and to which it is addressed, and it remains so to the very closing of Israel's Canon.

At the same time, Israel's theology is always, and in the most profound sense, historical. Every significant aspect of the faith of Israel is ultimately historically derived. But this is not to say that what Israel believes, she always believes from past to present. To be sure, Israel understands the meaning of God's activity in her present history in part in terms of her understanding of his activity in her past history. What *is* is interpreted by what *was*. But Israel's historical involvement also stimulates an opposite and simultaneous movement from present to past. The past is always subject to reinterpretation as the result of the interpretation of the present. What *was* is also interpreted by what *is*.

Israel conceives of no reality that is not historical reality. It is inevitable, therefore, that she clothe her primeval history in historical dress. What so convincingly to her *is* must have its expression in a setting of time and place and persons. The theological commentary on the relationship between universal God and universal man must have "historical" backgrounds if it is to have the realness which for Israel it so overwhelmingly has.

Israel understands that God tolls the bell and that when the bell tolls for one man, it tolls for all men.

II. LEGEND

Covenant with the Fathers: Genesis 12-50

He is Yahweh our God;
    his judgments are in all the earth
He is mindful of his covenant for ever,
    of the word that he commanded, for a thousand
      generations,
the covenant which he made with Abraham,
    his sworn promise to Isaac,
which he confirmed to Jacob as a statute,
    to Israel as an everlasting covenant. . . .

Ps. 105:7-10

A. ABRAHAM (GEN. 12-23)

What we read about Abraham is hardly the distillation of hero tales, for what is recalled in Genesis is not the exploits of Abraham but the initiative, the actions and the purpose of Yahweh in his relationship with Abraham. Yahweh *chose* Abraham. It is *his* election. *He* brought him forth from among the peoples. *He* initiated all that is intimately implied in the relationship between the namer and the one named. The judgment of Abraham's faithfulness was passed by Yahweh, not Abraham, nor Israel. Yahweh made the covenant.

Abraham is obviously not remembered here for the sake of the man Abraham, nor simply because of the relationship between God and that man. The Yahweh-Abraham cove-

60

nant is remembered not primarily for what *was* but what *is*. The people of Israel, the descendants of Abraham, read of themselves in the stories of their first patriarch. They understand the terms of their own existence, and its essential meaning, in the Yahweh-Abraham relationship.

1. *Election, Covenant and Response*

Like the primeval stories, the narratives about Abraham, Isaac, Jacob and Joseph are also confessional in character. They too articulate the faith of Israel, expressing what Israel essentially believes about herself in relation to the chasm between God and universal man. Israel answers the unresolved questions of the primeval story with a perfectly astounding affirmation: the problems of man's rebellion against God will be answered—and are in fact now being answered—by God's own initiative and action in human history in and through Abraham and the nation Israel—in whom all the families of the earth must ultimately be blessed.

This is the sense of Gen. 12:1-3. In the call of Abraham, Israel understands herself to have been called. The divine election of Abraham stands as a constant reminder of her own election. The promises to Abraham of significant nationhood and divine protection are promises to Israel. Israel need not say, "Let us make a name for ourselves" (11:4). Yahweh does this, for his own purposes: "I will . . . make your name great." What are the purposes? "So that you will be a blessing . . . in you all the families of the earth will be blessed." The very existence of Israel is explained, justified and defined in the three verses.

Israel also understands that Abraham's response is her own appropriate response to divine election.

Now the Lord said to Abram, "Go from your country and your kindred and your father's house to the land that I will show you."

[12:1]

So Abram went, as the Lord had told him.

[12:4]

This is faith, which alone makes possible the fulfillment of election purpose.

In chapter 15, the response of faith is again exemplified in Abraham. The patriarch is childless. The fulfillment of the promise requires an heir to the promise. When Abraham voices his anxiety,

behold, the word of the Lord came to him, ". . . your own son shall be your heir. . . . Look toward heaven, and number the stars, if you are able to number them. . . . So shall your descendants be."

And again, as in his call, Abraham responds in faith:

And he believed the Lord; and he reckoned it to him as righteousness.

It may be that Israel draws a significant comparison between Abraham and Noah. "Noah was a righteous man" (6:9), and yet the new beginning in righteousness came quickly to an abysmal failure in the continued evil of "the imagination of man's heart" (8:21). In contrast, we find no reason whatever given for the election of Abraham, nor anything to suggest that he merited the choice. In the full context of the Abraham stories, it can hardly be maintained that he was a righteous man. Faith, rather, is the distinguishing quality, which, as the stories (and the Bible) understand it, cannot in its very nature be primary, self-generated, meritorious. Faith is the response of trust to the divine initiative—and to the unrighteous Abraham (and therefore to Israel) faith is accounted as righteousness, faith becomes an attainable righteousness.

There follows now in chapter 15 an account, obviously ancient in origin, of the making of a covenant in which God in solemn, primitive symbol commits himself to the promises inherent in the election of Abraham. Abraham's response of faith in verse 6 has given way immediately—and as we shall see, characteristically—to unfaith, to doubt. Abraham asks in v. 8 how he shall know that he (his descendants) shall possess the land. He is told to sever three animals and place the severed halves opposite each other. Now,

When the sun had gone down and it was dark, behold, a smoking fire pot and a flaming torch passed between these pieces. On that day the Lord made a covenant with Abram. . . .

[15:17, 18]

There can be no doubt that the narrative means to represent Yahweh himself as passing between the pieces and as committing himself thereby in a binding ritual act. The rite suggests the probable origin of the most common Old Testament phrase for the making of a covenant, that is, literally, "to cut" a covenant. We know from documents recovered from the Hittite kingdom dating from the second millennium b.c. that covenants were sealed in the same symbolism;[1] and in Jer. 34:18 we are given to understand the seriousness of the commitment thus made:

Thus says the Lord [v. 17] . . . the men who transgressed my covenant and did not keep the terms of the covenant which they made before me, I will make like the calf which they cut in two and passed between its parts . . .

All of this is remarkably revealing of the faith of Israel. The covenant with Abraham in Gen. 15 is not of the type known among the Hittites, in which a vassal is bound by a king to certain obligations. Abraham is not yet asked to make any commitment on his part in return for the divine promises. It is not even a covenant in which both parties are bound. This is a one-way covenant, and it is the King, the Lord, who alone is bound, not the weaker party to the covenant!

Israel preserves and cherishes the account of Abraham's election in chapter 12, and reads in it her own experience of election in Egypt. In the story of chapter 15 in which Yahweh voluntarily binds himself, and himself alone, in covenant to Abraham, Israel reads her own experience of the exodus from Egypt, Yahweh's voluntary commitment to fulfill the promise inherent in Israel's election.

It is surely significant that in the arrangement of the stories about Abraham in Genesis, Abraham's own symbolic binding in covenant—to make of it, finally, a dual covenant —appears only after Yahweh has graciously sealed his own commitment. In chapter 17 Yahweh asks for the rite of circumcision as a sign of the covenant. Israel preserves here what she remembers to be the order of her own experience: it is only after election and exodus that she herself completes a two-way covenant at Sinai. It is the faith of Israel that she is asked to make her own commitment to Yahweh only after he has declared and demonstrated and sealed his own commitment. In the light of this belief we better understand how Israel's hope and faith in the ultimate fulfillment of the divine promise survived her own violation of the terms of the covenant and her destruction as a nation. The prior commitment was Yahweh's.

> He is the Lord our God;
>> his judgments are in all the earth
> He is mindful of his covenant for ever,
>> of the word that he commanded, for a thousand
>> generations,

the covenant which he made with Abraham,
    his sworn promise to Isaac,
which he confirmed to Jacob as a statute,
    to Israel as an everlasting covenant. . . .
                                    [Ps. 105:7-10]

The same covenant faith is expressed in Ps. 89, where the central figure is David.

If his children forsake my law
    and do not walk according to my ordinances,
if they violate my statutes
    and do not keep my commandments,
then I will punish their transgression with the rod
    and their iniquity with scourges;
but I will not remove from him [that is, Israel, seen
        corporately in the person of David] my stead-
        fast love,
    or be false to my faithfulness.
I will not violate my covenant,
    or alter the word that went forth from my lips.
                                    [Ps. 89:30-34]

2. *Tensions of the Covenant: Faith and Unfaith*

When Abraham acts in faith, he is a model of faith. His response in trust to the divine initiative is exemplary. The stories may well, then, reflect an idealizing tendency in Israel: we should respond in faith as did our father Abraham. It is a tendency, however, which has worked at best incompletely: for the cycle of stories about Abraham is liberally sprinkled with a knowing realism that seems to speak out of Israel's own experience under covenant.

The second important episode in the present arrangement of the narratives, following immediately upon the account of Abraham's call, response and consequent journey to Canaan, shows the great Patriarch, who has just acted with exemplary faith, behaving as if the divine promise had never occurred at all. Implicitly denying the validity of the promise of divine protection, he seeks to guarantee his own security during an emergency sojourn in Egypt (12:10 ff.). In perpetrating a lie about his wife (v. 13)—with obvious consequences for her (v. 15)—Abraham acts in gross unfaith. Israel reads her own experience in Abraham. Israel knows the response of faith. She also knows repeatedly in her historical existence the act which constitutes an unqualified denial of her faith.

This same tension between faith and unfaith is reflected elsewhere in the Abraham cycle, as well as in the stories of Isaac and Jacob. The essential plot of the story of the lie is repeated a second time of Abraham in chapter 20 where the scene is Gerar, not Egypt, and where, with a greater show of moral sensitivity, the story attempts to mitigate the patriarch's lie (v. 12) and maintain the sexual integrity of his wife (vv. 4-6). The plot appears a third time with Isaac as the lying patriarch in 26:6-11.

Again in effect denying his call, his election and his covenant promise, Abraham tries in other ways to take matters into his own hands. The divine promise of significant nationhood from his own progeny obviously demands an heir. But he and his wife are old and they have no son. The Hagar-Ishmael stories of chapter 16 and chapter 21:7-21 represent another aspect of the tension between faith and unfaith. Despairing of the fulfillment of the promise, Abraham and Sarah attempt to actualize the promise themselves through Sarah's maid, Hagar (16:2 ff.), with the unhappy results of Sarah's jealousy and the brutal expulsion of Hagar. In the second Hagar story, Sarah's own child, Isaac, is born (21:2) but even this evidence of the validity of the divine promise is not enough: in gross unfaith, again, Sarah insists and Abraham acquiesces in the expulsion of Hagar and her son

Ishmael. Sarah's words convey the denial of God's power to bring the promise to fulfillment:

Cast out this slave woman with her son; for the son of this slave woman shall not be heir with my son Isaac.

[21:10]

Here, too, Israel reads her own experience of seeking to take matters of the covenant, the Yahweh covenant, into her own hands, to force, by her own means, in her own way, in trust in her own devices, the fulfillment of the divine promise. Most tellingly, Abraham responds in bald distrust when, before Isaac is born, he laughs with derisive denial in—as it were—the very face of God!

And God said to Abraham . . . "I will bless her [Sarah], and . . . she shall be a mother of nations; kings of peoples shall come from her." Then Abraham fell on his face and laughed, and said to himself, "Shall a child be born to a man who is a hundred years old? Shall Sarah, who is ninety years old, bear a child?"

[17:15-17]

The stories of Abraham take their pattern from the experience of Israel, but they also speak instructively back to that same experience, illustrating not only the way of faith—but the way also of unfaith. The tension that Israel knew throughout her life as a nation between faith in an electing, acting, covenanting God on the one hand, and on the other the rational improbability, if not absurdity, of the divine promises implicit in her faith; the conflict between the divine demand to trust and the human doubt; the incongruity between divine promise for the nation and the incredible historical odds against fulfillment—all of this Israel is mindful of in the shaping of the stories, and in the reading and cherishing of the stories. Yet the final thrust of the Abraham cycle of stories is in substantiation of faith: the incredible happened to Abraham, the impossible occurred; and it occurred—how reassuring to rebellious Israel—in spite of the patriarch's acts of unfaith! It is God who initiates. It is he who has spoken. He has committed himself to the covenant.

3. *The Climax and Resolution of Tension*

Nevertheless, the divine demand for the human response of faith remains. The promise thaws and dissolves itself into a dew without faith. Israel's persistent, obstinate hope in the ultimate fulfillment of the promise is itself an act of faith, made defiantly in the face of her own repeated abandonment of faith. The only substance of the promise is in faith.

The story of the near-sacrifice of Isaac in chapter 22 is at once the climax and the resolution of the tension. It is a story told with consummate economy and skill. No word is wasted. Simplicity is the effective instrument of its power. Pathos is conveyed with no reference at all, no single word, descriptive of the emotions of father or son, but rather in dialogue and in chaste narration. In the call of Abraham (12:1), the magnitude of the demand appears in the simple enumeration of what Abraham must voluntarily surrender:

> Go from
> > your country and
> > your kindred and
> > your father's house
> > [where?]
> to the land *that I will show you* [!]

Here, in 22:1 f., the absolute totality of what faith is asked to surrender is similarly expressed:

After these things God tested Abraham, and said to him "Abraham!" And he said, "Here am I."

He [God] said, "Take
your son,
your only son
Isaac [the name!]
whom you love

... and offer him there [in the land of Moriah] as a burnt offering
[where?]
upon one of the mountains *of which I shall tell you.* [vv. 6b-8] ...
So they went both of them together. And Isaac said to his father
Abraham, "My father!" And he said, "Here am I, my son." He
said, "Behold, the fire and the wood; but where is the lamb for a
burnt offering?" Abraham said, "God will provide himself the
lamb for a burnt offering, my son." So they went both of them
together.

This is a story that maintains its literary power under the
eyes of any reader, in any interpretation. But we suspect that
the content of the narrative breaks down into absurdity
except when it is read with the eyes of Israel's faith, as an
expression of what Israel understands to be the necessary
totality of the response of faith. Like Abraham, Israel made
a partial response of faith in breaking with the past and
setting forth from Egypt for a land "that I will show you."
Like Abraham, she had known immediate doubt and had
sought to take matters into her own hands. Like Abraham,
she believed that the enterprise was divinely initiated, divinely covenanted; and like him, she accepted and symbolized her own commitment to the covenant. But in every
crisis of her history she suffered *what she inevitably read
into* the story of the near-sacrifice of Isaac: the only tangible
means of the fulfillment of the promise, preposterously
achieved (to be sure, only by the mighty acts of God), the
only visible hope for ultimate fulfillment—in the case of
Abraham, Isaac; in the case of Israel, her very historical

existence—this she is asked to be willing to sacrifice. Destroy in faith the only concrete evidence that faith can be fulfilled!

Israel here comes very close to affirming precisely what is affirmed in the New Testament community of faith:

> For whoever would save his life will lose it, and whoever loses his life for my sake will find it.
>
> > [Matt 16:25; see Mark 8:35 and Luke 9:24]

This brings to a climax the tension between faith and unfaith. It points to, and illustrates, the only resolution of the tension—the complete and unqualified response of faith. We do not find the resolution historically enacted in and by Israel. The tension between faith and unfaith continued: the commitment of faith remained only partial. Israel's prophets understood the nation's destruction and exile as the result of unfaith, the taking of matters of the covenant into her own hands, the failure to make the total commitment of faith. The prophet Isaiah, in the latter part of the eighth century B.C., put it this way:

> If you will not believe,
>   surely you shall not be established.
>
> > [7:9b]
>
> For thus said the Lord God, the Holy One of Israel,
>   "In returning and rest you shall be saved;
>   in quietness and *in trust* shall be your strength."
> And you would not. . . .
>
> > [30:15]

Israel understands the story of the near-sacrifice of Isaac to say: Except we be willing to lose our life for Yahweh's sake, we shall neither find nor save our life. The demand of faith is total. The response of faith must be unqualified, complete.

This is the climax of the Abraham cycle of stories. The narrative moves quickly now through the death of Sarah and the purchase of the cave of Machpelah (chapter 23) to the altogether charming story of Isaac's successful quest for a wife (24), the last days and death of Abraham (25:1 ff.) and the introduction of Jacob, the central figure in the next significant cycle of stories in Genesis (25:19 ff.).

B. MYTH, LEGEND AND HISTORY

We have thus far looked at the stories about Abraham, and only at parts of the cycle, with empathy, from within, as we think Israel herself shaped, read, understood and interpreted the stories. This is also the way in which, primarily, we surveyed Gen. 1-11. But again, as there, questions inevitably arise out of the intellectual disposition of our own environment of the twentieth-century West. We are struck by an obvious difference between primeval and patriarchal stories: they differ in quality—they are not of the same literary stuff. Gen. 12-50 often returns the impression of reality, of flesh and blood in time and history. Some of this, in contrast to the first eleven chapters of Genesis, *could* have happened. Places frequented by Abraham and Jacob can be located—Mamre, Hebron, Bethel, Shechem, Dothan (all in the central hill country of Palestine) and Beer-sheba (in the south). Some of the personal names in Gen. 11:16 ff. were names of towns in the general area of Haran, Abraham's immediate point of origin (11:31 f.): Peleg, Serug, Nahor and Terah. What is described in the Patriarchal narratives purports to have occurred in literary, historical times, not preliterate prehistorical times. If we have no direct extrabiblical confirmation of Abraham and Jacob, we find, nevertheless, a remarkable correlation between what is reflected in the stories about their backgrounds and what we learn of life in the ancient Near East in the first half of the second millennium B.C.

The general credibility of the patriarchal backgrounds is greatly enhanced by archaeological discoveries. We know that the fertile lands of the Near East were overrun during several centuries following about 2000 B.C. by desert invaders—the same groups referred to in the Old Testament as Amorites. We suspect that Abraham's migrations, and perhaps Jacob's, are a part of this widespread Amorite movement, and in two archaeological finds, in particular, we find conditions of life described in terms remarkably similar to those of Abraham and Jacob. In the Tale of Sinuhe, dating from about 1900 B.C., an Egyptian official of that name is forcibly exiled and takes refuge with an Amorite chieftain. The seminomadic life described with considerable color and detail accords very well with that of the patriarchal stories. A more important discovery was made in 1937 at Mari, the capital of an extensive Amorite kingdom stretching in the eighteenth century B.C. from near Babylon in the east to Syria in the west. Thousands of clay documents were recovered from the archives of one of Mari's kings in that century, including several letters from a variety of people and places scattered over Syria and Mesopotamia. And, again, what is reflected here of life in the eighteenth century agrees remarkably with what is depicted in the Genesis narratives about Abraham, Isaac and Jacob.

At least two other finds tend to confirm the general accuracy of the patriarchal backgrounds. The Nuzi (or Nuzu) texts, discovered in an Assyrian town of that name, are largely concerned with business matters of the fifteenth century, and contain some significant parallels to episodes recorded in Genesis. The Ugarit texts, from Ras Shamrah on the Syrian coast, deal for the most part with Canaanite religion prior to Israel's settlement in the land. They are important because they show rather conclusively that certain

Mesopotamian aspects of Israel's life and thought were not—as was believed previous to their discovery—mediated through the Canaanites, since there is no hint of them in this material, but must rather have come directly from Mesopotamia. This tends to confirm the tradition of the patriarchs that they maintained direct associations with Mesopotamia.

All of this is to say that there is a credibility about the Abraham-Isaac-Jacob cycles of stories—a credibility that tends to be confirmed by archaeology. But this is not to say that we therefore accept the stories as literally factual and accurate. We certainly cannot take as sober history or straight reporting, such things as these:

Abraham fears Sarah's beauty as a threat to his own safety when she is over sixty-five and again when she is past ninety (12 and 20)

He laughs at the idea of having a son at the age of ninety-nine (17:17), but forty years later, without so much as batting an eye, he marries Keturah and apparently accepts the subsequent offspring in stride (25:1 ff.)

The Amalekites are represented as settled in southern Palestine in Abraham's time (14:7); yet Amalek himself, who presumably founded the clan, is a grandson of Esau who in turn is the grandson of Abraham.

And this is only to illustrate the relatively common occurrence of incongruity, anachronism, exaggeration and discrepancy in the patriarchal stories. To say that the general backgrounds, the local color, the atmosphere of the environment, and even the existence of the patriarchs—to say that this is to the best of our knowledge true is not, on the other hand, to say that the stories are, in the usual sense of the word, history.

The term "history" is commonly used of written accounts of public events recorded upon reliable contemporary evidence. But, with the exception of Gen. 14, and possibly certain aspects of the Joseph story, we simply are not dealing in Gen. 12-50 with public events but almost entirely with private affairs of a domestic and sometimes intimate nature. Details of private meetings, conversations and family frictions are not the stuff of history. In the main, we may say that Genesis is comprised of two literary forms. The first eleven chapters are chiefly *myth;* and the stories of Abraham, Isaac, Jacob and Joseph are best termed *legend.* By the term "myth" we mean to convey our understanding that what is narrated is not a literal occurrence of the past; and by legend, that the story probably has a basis in an actual person or occurrence of the past.[2]

But this is certainly not to say that myth and legend are in a broader sense of the word "unhistorical." If we understand history as that which belongs to the past and which throws light upon the past, then myth and legend have a high historical value. If neither is strictly a factual account of that with which in narrative form it is concerned, both myth and legend may be *true*—and demonstrably are in Genesis—in reflecting the mind, the aspirations, the hopes and fears and beliefs of the peoples among whom they circulated. The myths of Genesis tell us, as no objective history of public events could, what the community of Israel essentially believed about God's relationship to the world and to man; and the legends of the Fathers record Israel's understanding of herself, her own relationship to God and the world, her own sense of sin and inadequacy in tension with her conviction of special divine Election, her fears on the one hand and her highest hopes on the other. Supremely the myths and legends of Genesis tell us of the faith of Israel, of what this continuing community believed about God not

abstractly but in his active relationship to world and Israelite history.

It may be that we fail rightly to understand legend and
its relationship to history because we have not rightly understood history, and perhaps particularly, biblical history. No
true history is mere reporting. No true historian can avoid
interpreting the past: he reconstructs and tells the story of
the past because it is relevant and instructive to the present,
and he must tell it in such a way that it is intelligible to the
present. History, as well as legend, is concerned with the
relationship of the past and the present. And in the Old
Testament, history and legend *and myth* are in peculiar
affinity because all three are first concerned to tell, not of
man's, but of God's activity. Whatever the original intent
of Old Testament myth and legend, it is shaped, preserved
and understood in Israel by faith. So, precisely, Israel also
remembers, records and interprets her history by faith.

We must ask, then, How are legend and history different?
They differ in two respects, chiefly; that is, in the *manner* in
which they visualize the past, and in the *matters* with which
they are in the main concerned. Legend and history take
form in two highly differentiated strata in the life of Israel.
We do not necessarily infer that legend is early and history
late, for legend and history may develop simultaneously
around the same subject, as they apparently do, for example,
in the case of the prophet Elijah, in the ninth century. We
simply mean that legend looks at the past, distant or near,
and retells it in a spontaneous and intuitive manner. Legend, no less than history, remembers the past; but it remembers it with a creative abandon, in disregard of history's
concern, always present whatever the degree of interpretation, to give a rational and coherent reconstruction. The
factors of spontaneity and intuition in legend bring into

focus other matters than those upon which history chiefly concentrates. Old Testament history recounts events, the lives of great men, prophets, priests and kings, migrations, wars, political decisions—everything affecting the *exterior* life of the nation, the observable course of her turbulent history. Legend treats the *interior* history, related, to be sure, but not the same. It tells the inner history of Israel's fears and hopes, the realities and aspirations of her existence, what she thinks and knows herself to be on the one hand, and what she believes that she may be on the other. It tells, in short, the inner history of her life with God.[3]

It follows that in legend what is past is only apparently so, or perhaps rather that if the past is past it is also present. Distinctions in time, the measure of time, and the correlation of time and event are, if not obliterated, reduced to insignificance. Legend retains from the rubrics of history only the concern for sequence; yet in legend it is always a sequence determined not by past event but by present faith. The legends of Gen. 12-50 *may* recall in major outline an actual sequence; but it is certain that the order and arrangement of the stories correspond to the inner story, the sequence as faith dictates sequence. Old Testament *history* consistently understands and interprets the present from the past; and if, thus, the past is in the present, its meaning for the present is precisely because it is past—by what God has *done* Israel understands what God is doing and what he will do. Legend does not make history's distinction in tenses. The past has meaning not for its "wasness" but for its "isness" and it is therefore the power of legend to reduce into a single episode—Gen. 22, for example—the progress, experience and heritage of centuries of faith.

All of this is to say, then, that myth and legend in the Old Testament serve for us a historical purpose: the literature of Genesis informs us in a unique way about the faith of the community of Israel, about what Israel believed.

We cannot, however, fail to observe certain characteristics of legend which do not contribute directly to this purpose. If, in Genesis, individual legends and originally separate cycles of legends are combined in such a way as to convey the theological drama of Israel, if the spoken lines are the lines of the play, we observe at the same time that this literary material of legend always refuses to yield itself completely to such editorial, theological design. It insists on maintaining at the same time its own identity—that is, if the characters do speak the lines of the theological drama, they also continue to speak their own lines as well. If Abraham and Jacob are Israel in the first millennium B.C., they are also Abraham and Jacob of the second millennium B.C. If the stories convey an "isness" they continue to convey a "wasness." Particularly at certain points, we sense the oral quality of the stories: this, or this, or this strikes us as something *told*, even though we *read* it now. We become part of a listening group, with a group sensitivity. Here we sense satisfaction in a good story for the sake of a good story and pleasure in the qualities of a good story precisely because they contribute to a good story—the well-turned phrase, tension and suspense, eloquent dialogue, repartee, and even humor. All of this appears in the Lot-Abraham cycle in chapters 13-14 and 18-19; and we should be dull indeed if we missed in chapter 23 the pleasure both of the teller and the hearer in the humor of the exceedingly polite negotiations over the purchase of the cave of Machpelah. One of the best examples of the use of humor in legend occurs in the next chapter. Abraham, now a man of great wealth, sends one of his servants back to his old homeland, Nahor near Haran, to find a wife for his son Isaac. The servant takes with him gifts appropriate to the wealth of his master, and when he finds Rebekah, he presents her with a ring and bracelets of impressive value, and asks for hospitality. Rebekah runs home; and what has been a story told with beautiful simplicity and effective description now is artfully relieved in humor at Laban's expense. When Laban, Rebekah's brother,

saw the ring, and the bracelets on his sister's arms . . . he said [to Abraham's servant], "Come in, O blessed of the Lord; why do you stand outside?"

There is obvious pleasure in the stories for their qualities simply as good stories. We cannot but note also that the legends of Genesis, like the myths, still bear the signs of frequent etiological influence and motivation. Legend, too, is interested in the explanation of existing phenomena in terms of origin. Most of the legends of Genesis can, in fact, be classified according to etiological type.

1. The *ethnological* legend arises to account for—which generally means to give the origin of—the characteristics and nature and geography relating to known tribes and ethnic groups. For example, the fact that the descendants of Lot, Ammon and Moab (ch. 19), are not in Palestine but in the more barren territory to the East and South is a phenomenon explained in the division of the territory between Abraham and Lot (ch. 13). Underlying many of the legends is a central ethnological theme—the explanation of how the people of Israel rightfully possess the land of Canaan.

2. The *etymological* legend explaining the origin of names is also common in Genesis. We have already indicated the great significance attached to names in Israel, and indeed among all ancient peoples. Because the name is one with the essence of the thing named great care and ceremony were

exercised in the giving of names; and we find reflected in the legends of Genesis an inordinate interest in the origin of ancient names of both places and people. The explanation of Isaac's name (from a word meaning "laughter") is indicated in the thrice-repeated narrative motif of laughter over the idea and fact of Isaac's birth (17:17, 18:12, 21:6). So is Ishmael's (16:11, 17:20, 21:17). The meaning "heelholder" is given to the name Jacob with the explanation that he was born holding his twin brother by the heel (25:26). The town of Zoar (trifle) got its name because Lot pleaded with Yahweh for its preservation on the ground that it was "a little one" (19:20). There are yet other instances in Genesis where the legend may properly be classified as etymological, or where one aspect of the legend has to do with the meaning of a name.

3. The *cult* legend accounts for the sacredness of a sanctuary or a ritual act or custom. Thus, all of the major sanctuaries of Israel are associated with experiences of the patriarchs, as, for example, Jacob at Bethel (28:10 ff.). The rite of circumcision, attributed in its origin to Abraham in Gen. 17 is elsewhere associated with Moses (Exod. 4:24-26) and again, apparently, with Joshua (Josh. 5:2 ff.) although here it is recognized that this is not the first occasion.[4]

If the legends of Genesis have been employed editorially in such a way as to express the faith of Israel and if, in the legends of the patriarchs, Israel sees her own experience mirrored, it is also true that the legends retain at the same time their own stamp, something of their own unique character. The appreciation of the qualities of entertainment and the recognition of the major etiological motives help us to understand the origin and nature of the legend in Israel.

Before leaving the Abraham cycle of stories and this general discussion of myth, legend and history, two other items

appear for brief consideration. The first has to do with the
introduction in the Abraham cycle of what scholars have
long regarded as a third source in Genesis (with J and P),
the E document (later than J; so called because of its prefer-
ence for the divine name *elohim*). The source appears for
the first time probably at chapter 15 and is illustrated at its
best in the second Hagar episode (21:8-21; the first, in chapter 16, is usually ascribed to J) and in the story of the near-
sacrifice of Isaac (22).[5]

The second item has to do with chapter 14, which has
been for years and remains a literary and historical enigma.
We can easily understand its incorporation: it redounds in
every way to Abraham's credit and favor; and the Melchizedek episode, vv. 17 ff., clearly had pointed significance in
Israel after the establishment of Jerusalem as the capital by
David and the building of Solomon's temple (Salem, v. 18, =
Jerusalem; Melchizedek is not only king, but "priest of the
God most high" to whom Abraham gives "a tenth of everything"). The later Temple tax (tithe = tenth) is here given
ultimate precedent and example in Abraham. But the chapter defies literary classification, betraying none of the common characteristics of J or P or E; all attempts to give
positive identification to the kings named in vv. 1 and 2 have
thus far failed; and the historical accuracy of the account
continues in question.

C. THE JACOB CYCLE (GEN. 24-36, 38)

The character of Isaac is hardly sufficiently drawn to return an impression of independence; or perhaps it would be
better to say that the stories about Isaac appear more as a
link between the Abraham and Jacob cycles than as an independent unit of stories. In chapter 24, which tells how
Rebekah is found and brought to Isaac, the chief character

is Abraham's servant, and what transpires is for the most part in the name of Abraham. After considerations of a statistical nature, chapter 25 moves to the birth of Jacob and Esau and Esau's sacrifice (or Jacob's theft) of the birthright. It is only chapter 26 which features Isaac, yet what we find here, among other things, is a story of Isaac's denial of Rebekah's true relationship to him (already twice told of Abraham and Sarah, in chs. 12 and 20), and a repetition of the divine promise to Abraham, *in the name of Abraham*:

I am the God of Abraham your father; fear not, for I am with you and will bless you and multiply your descendants for my servant Abraham's sake.

[26:24, but see also vv. 1-5]

Yet another motif carried over from Abraham is that of the barren wife:

And Isaac prayed to the Lord for his wife, because she was barren; and the Lord granted his prayer. . . .

[25:21]

Isaac is a link between Abraham and Jacob, repeating and transmitting the essential character of the patriarch as the man of divine promise. Isaac acts in faith and implicitly understands that he bears the covenant. Yet, having acted in faith, and having received offspring as a tangible evidence of the promise at work, he, like his father, acts in unfaith (26:7) immediately following the virtual repetition of the full promise made to Abraham (26:3 f.): he, too, attempts to insure his own safety, his own security. It is hardly accidental that the story of the denial of the wife is repeated three times: Israel thus underlines her own repeated effort to take the divine promise into her own hands and to manipulate its fulfillment.

We have already suggested that the idealizing tendency,

common to legend in general, is conspicuously weak in the stories of the patriarchs. We see suggestions of the tendency at work in the Abraham cycle to shape the character of the Patriarch to the pattern of faith, the ideal of faith. But the tendency fails. The cycle is pervaded by a realism derived, we suspect, in part from contact with historical reality and in part from Israel's realistic reading of her own experience and her own character in the Abraham stories.

1. *The Jacob Stories and the Faith of Israel*

The cycle of stories which revolves around the character of Jacob differs from that of Abraham. If the idealizing tendency has had only a partial influence on the Abraham material, it is almost totally absent in the Jacob stories. Jacob is presented with a singularly high degree of realism. We find little, if any, effort to "improve" the character of Jacob: no word or phrase appears to relieve his premeditated treachery against his father Isaac (27:1 ff.), and his twin brother Esau (25:29 ff. and 27:30 ff.). Even in the scene of their reconciliation, Jacob is guilty of rank deceit of Esau. When Jacob returns to Canaan after an absence of twenty years and is met on his way by a forgiving Esau, Jacob agrees to take up his residence beside his brother in the south of the land, in Seir.

So Esau returned that day on his way to Seir. *But Jacob journeyed to Succoth,* and built himself a house. . . .

[33:16 f.]

When we add to this the detailed description of Jacob's unmitigated crime against Laban (30:25 ff.), we are not putting it too strongly when we say that Jacob is depicted, quite candidly, as a disreputable character.

Why is this so? If, as we suspect, the myths and legends

of Genesis are shaped by Israel's faith, what does this mean?
The Abraham stories are pointed to the climax of the account
of the near-sacrifice of Isaac, the ideal response of faith. Why
is the corresponding point in the Jacob cycle the story of the
patriarch's violent, night-long wrestling bout with the deity,
and his refusal to surrender even to the very end of the
struggle (32:22-30)?

Can it be that the two cycles of stories come to their final
form with two different historical epochs in mind? Abraham
strikingly personifies the era of Israel's historical beginnings,
the time of Moses and the Exodus.[6] The cycle bears a particular correspondence to that first dramatic epoch in Israel's
life without which, indeed, there would never have been an
Israel. Like Abraham, Israel is called by Yahweh out of the
known and the familiar, to the unknown and the strange, to
a land that only Yahweh knows. Like Abraham, Israel is
elected in her first historical epoch to an unseen destiny
whose only substance is in divine promise. Like Abraham,
Israel made, in Egypt, the response of faith: she demonstrated there her readiness to lose her life in order to find it.
Like him, she knew even in that first and most glorious phase
of her life the tension between faith and unfaith, the inescapable temptation to take matters of divine promise into
her own hands. And as also in the case of Abraham, these
tensions were resolved at length in an act of faith which
resulted in the partial substantiation of the promise—the
acquisition of a land.

With the acquisition of the land Israel becomes Israel,
the nation Israel. And Jacob *is* Israel. The account of the
changing of Jacob's name to Israel is twice given, once from
J (32:28) and again from P (35:10). Recall the significance
in Israel of the name, the psychological content of meaning
given in Israel to the relationship between the Namer and

the one named; and recall, too, that the name is of the essence of the object named. Jacob is Jacob-*Israel*: Israel is *Jacob*-Israel. The nation Israel is of the same essence as the man Israel. If the Abraham stories are shaped by the first phase of Israel's history, that phase in which Israel became Israel, and if they are read and interpreted in Israel as a personalized account of her formative faith in her formative event, we may well wonder whether there is not a corresponding relationship between the Jacob stories and the middle phase of her history, the era of her autonomous existence in her own land, on her own soil. We will presently raise the possibility of a similar relationship between the Joseph story and the third and final phase of her history in the Old Testament.

The sense of such correspondence may have been as much unconscious as conscious. That it was there we have no doubt. That it informs us richly of what Israel believed about herself we are certain. Israel believed herself to be divinely elected, chosen by Yahweh for purposes fully known only to himself. But the Jacob stories emphasize a central point of interpretation: Israel's election is understood not as merited or earned, but as the free choice of Yahweh, for *reasons* known only to himself. Election and the covenant remain a reality not by virtue of what Israel is, and how she behaves in her history, but simply by virtue of the grace and love of God. This is the central meaning of the stories about Jacob. It is an emphasis which the great prophets powerfully and eloquently reiterate.

We see this theme expressed in several ways in the Jacob cycle. In the ancient East pre-eminence is naturally given—or naturally expected to fall upon—the older son, or the eldest son. This is the normal expectation. Jacob, although a twin, is the younger brother. But here is the mystery and freedom of God's way in election: the lesser vehicle, Jacob-

Israel, bears the promise and the blessing. And this is a point of emphasis in Israel by no means confined to Jacob. Preeminence is also the lot of Joseph, Gideon (Judg. 6:15), David and Solomon, all, to name only a few, younger sons. It is surely in part this same quality of election which the apostle Paul had in mind in the New Testament when he wrote:

> God chose what is foolish in the world to shame the wise, God chose what is weak in the world to shame the strong. God chose what is low and despised in the world, even things that are not, to bring to nothing things that are, so that no human being might boast in the presence of God.
>
> [I Cor. 1:27-29]

In shaping and preserving and cherishing the stories of Jacob as her own story, Israel understood that it was *God's* election, in which she had no cause to boast.

In the realistic portrayal of the character of Jacob, Israel sees herself portrayed; and she is reminded again in the portrayal that election is certainly not ethically and morally merited. Jacob-Israel is no Galahad, whose strength is in purity of heart. Election is hers not because of any intrinsic goodness and nobility of her own, but rather, as it would appear, despite the deviousness of her ways, in the grace and purpose of God. It is precisely here that the Jacob cycle expresses its own peculiar tension, comparable to the tension between faith and unfaith that characterizes the Abraham cycle. It is a tension between human perversity and divine purpose, between human sin and divine grace. It is a tension precisely articulated later in the Joseph narrative when Joseph, reunited with his treacherous brothers, declares, "You meant evil against me; but God meant it for good" (50:20).

Or, to use a more graphic figure, we may say that the Jacob narrative in its present unified structure is internally

supported like a bridge, on two pillars—the accounts of
Jacob at Bethel (28:10 ff.) and at Peniel (32:22 ff.).[7] The
story of Jacob's vision of the ladder at Bethel and the accompanying detailed repetition of the divine promise and
blessing follow immediately upon the accounts of Jacob's
underhanded acquisition of his brother's birthright (25), his
subsequent bald treachery in securing the first-born's blessing (ch. 27—Jacob does not figure at all in ch. 26), and his
ignominious flight from home before the wrath of his brother
(27:41-45). And now, with an abruptness that itself emphasized the mystery and freedom of divine action, Jacob receives the blessing of God apparently on his first stop away
from home. The mantle of Abraham and Isaac's blessing is
placed around Jacob, with the added words,

Behold, I am with you and will keep you wherever you go, and
will bring you back to this land; for I will not leave you until
I have done that of which I have spoken to you.

[28:15]

If Israel read the shame of her own sinfulness in the sins of
Jacob, she also understood that the divine promise to Jacob
was the promise of Yahweh to Israel.

There follows the story of a Jacob now bent on the acquisition of wealth, determined and unprincipled enough to
get it at any cost. He carries through a systematic twenty-
year operation in which Laban, his father-in-law (or brother-
in-law—and no mean competitor, he!), is completely fleeced.
With virtually all of Laban's wealth successfully acquired in
chapter 30, the second verse of the next chapter stands as a
remarkable understatement:

And Jacob saw that Laban did not regard him with favor as
before [!].

[31:2]

Again Jacob is forced to flee, this time in the opposite direction. With his treachery against Laban just behind him, and
the awful reminder of his shame against father and brother
just ahead in the inevitable meeting with Esau, God falls
upon him as a nocturnal spirit who, after a struggle that
endures throughout the night, again gives—this time simply
in a name—both promise and blessing:

> Your name shall no more be called Jacob, but Israel [that is,
> "He who strives with God" or "God strives"], for you have striven
> with God and with men, and have prevailed.
>
> [32:28]

Remembering that the faith of Israel is portrayed in the
legends of Genesis primarily by the selection and arrangement of narratives which had an independent and often
ancient origin, we need not wonder that the story of Peniel
retains something of the enigmatic and primitive from its
origin. But the editorial intention is clear. This is the second
pillar of faith, supporting the bridge of the Jacob narrative.
Remove the two pillars of Bethel and Peniel, and the whole
structure collapses. Jacob is—Jacob. In and of himself he is
treacherous, deceitful, acquisitive, prideful and self-centered.
He cannot even make the response of faith that Abraham
did: at Bethel the admission is wrung from his lips, "Surely
Yahweh is in this place; *and I did not know it*"; and at Peniel
he is uncertain even of the identity of his visitor and fights
all night against Yahweh.

The story of Jacob is supported only by divine grace, only
by divine intention and purpose. Or, to return to a description of the Jacob cycle in terms of tension, it is characterized
by a tension between human perversity and divine grace, a
tension resolved only in the obvious final inequality of any

contest between man and God. God can take even the evil
intention of man and convert it to good, if he so wills.

So, in the long central phase of her history from the
acquisition to the loss of the land, Israel is—Israel. Nor can
she make, save only sporadically, the response of faith which
she herself had made in that first phase of her history, as
her prophets are wont to remind her. Israel's history too is
a story of sustained tension between her own perversity and
the purpose of God: hers, too is a history which she herself
understands to be supported only by the grace of God, and
his purpose for her declared of old that in her all the families
of the earth should be blessed. This is the story of Jacob;
but he is Jacob-Israel and it is also the story of Israel.

2. *The Jacob Stories as Literature and History*

Like the primeval history, like the Abraham cycle, the
Jacob narratives are shaped by faith. But there are prior
levels of interpretation, again, which we cannot ignore. The
individual stories still speak at points with qualities of expression characteristic of their origin and background in
ancient folklore, when the stories were primarily motivated
by etiology of one sort or another, or by the love, simply, of
a good story, or by the desire to entertain and to be enter-
tained. In the Abraham stories we detect, among other
motives, the desire to validate Israel's claim to the land of
Canaan. This remains a strong implication of the story of
the quarrel between Lot (the father of the nations Moab
and Ammon) and Abraham, and Lot's free *choice* of the
land to the east and south of Canaan proper (13). The same
motive partially underlies the repeated promise of the land
to Abraham, Isaac and Jacob and the pointed denial of the
claims of others, for example Ishmael (the Ishmaelites) and
Esau (the Edomites) as well as Moab and Ammon. As in the
Abraham stories, so too in the Jacob narratives, the sacred-

ness and often the very name of ancient Canaanite sanctuaries are attributed to the visit of a patriarch to the scene, as witness, only for example, the stories of Bethel (28) and Peniel (32). This too contributes somewhat more subtly to the validation of Israel's claim.

We assume that many of the stories circulated orally before they came to be recorded in writing; and again we sense the pleasure and response of the listening group to the well-told and well-executed tale, to the lyrical phrase, or to the effective description. *Listen* to these lines for their chasteness, their descriptive power, or their sheer beauty—and this is in translation!

> . . . Esau was a skilful hunter, a man of the field, while Jacob was a quiet man, dwelling in tents. Isaac loved Esau, because he ate of his game; but Rebekah loved Jacob.
>
> > [25:27 f.]

From Isaac's blessing of Jacob:

> See, the smell of my son
> > is as the smell of a field which the Lord
> > > has blessed!
> May God give you of the dew of heaven,
> > and of the fatness of the earth. . . .
> > > [27:27b f.]

This *word* of blessing, solemnly spoken, cannot be recalled. It is a dynamic word, releasing the power of accomplishment, even though intended for the first born. It is thus that we understand the weight of anguish in the negative parallelism of Isaac's blessing of Esau:

> Behold, away from the fatness of the earth
> > shall your dwelling be,
> > and away from the dew of heaven on high.
> > > [27:39]

Hear, too, this line so simply but eloquently descriptive of the love of a man for a maid:

Jacob served seven years for Rachel, and they seemed to him but a few days because of the love he had for her.

[29:20]

Sympathy of storyteller and listener for the unloved Leah is implicated in a single line put on her lips when she bears her first child:

When Yahweh saw that Leah was hated, he opened her womb . . . and she said . . . surely *now* my husband will love me.

[29:31 f.]

And in the meeting between Jacob and Esau, when Jacob approaches filled with apprehension, remembering his earlier deceit, and about to deceive again, it is Esau who steals the scene with an unqualified expression of forgiveness and affection:

Esau ran to meet him, and embraced him, and fell on his neck and kissed him, and they wept.

[33:4]

And listening to the story, we all understand that while one wept simply in the release of personal apprehension, the other wept in love.

Although the individual stories are employed and arranged editorially for a serious overall purpose, we can still hear in some of them the sound of laughter. If faith gives form to the structure of the stories of Genesis, and if the stories are therefore instructive to the continuing faith of Israel, it is also clear that Israel, early and late, *enjoyed* the narratives of the fathers. They laughed at Laban, the acquisitive Laban, running forth to greet the representative of the wealthy house of Abraham (24:29 ff.) . They laughed again when the eager performance was repeated by the same man with the current heir, Jacob. Recalling, as it were, the financial rating of the family, Laban

ran to meet him, and embraced him and kissed him, and brought him to his house . . . and Laban said to him, "Surely you are my bone and my flesh!"

[29:13 f.]

Earlier, when Jacob first arrives in the country of Laban, he comes upon a well covered by a large stone which can be removed only by the assembled strength of a host of shepherds. But

when Jacob saw Rachel the daughter of Laban his mother's brother, and the sheep of Laban his mother's brother [Jacob and Laban have a lot in common!], Jacob went up and rolled the stone from the well's mouth. . . .

[29:10]

The whole thing was a very taxing emotional experience. In the next verse we read:

Jacob kissed Rachel, and wept aloud.

These stories were told and heard, recorded and read— and enjoyed! The composition of the stories into a structure now reflecting profound meditation on the meaning of history and the nature and activity of God in history has not obscured a zestful appreciation of the life that produced the stories. Words, phrases and individual narratives may have a kind of *double-entendre*. As we have earlier remarked, the characters in Genesis speak their own lines, lines in immediate contact with the realities of their own existence, as well as the lines of the theological drama of God's concern in love to reconcile man and himself. And this is to distinguish the very essence of biblical religion: it is never detached and speculative, it is never theoretical. Myth, to be meaningful, must be given historical setting, with names, and places, and even genealogies. Legend is always in contact with historical reality. And history, interpreted in faith, as to be sure it always is, is nevertheless always history— blood, sweat and tears, the full spectrum of earthiness, given meaning and purpose in the activity of God in the same earthy arena! Precisely this is why passing generations in all the passing centuries have found the Bible to be relevant.

Granting the absence of shorthand in the first half of the second millennium B.C., granting that detailed objective reality undergoes distortion in the mold of popular legend, granting that etiology is not science and that oral tradition is not scientific history—granting all of this, we may nevertheless reiterate what we have already affirmed in discussing the Abraham cycle of stories, but in words vastly more authoritative than our own:

It is . . . uncertain to what extent we can adopt the traditional order of events or the precise motivation attributed to them. Nor can we accept every picturesque detail as it stands in our present narrative. But as a whole the picture in Genesis [of the Patriarchs] is historical, and there is no reason to doubt the general accuracy of the biographical details and the sketches of personality which make the Patriarchs come alive with a vividness unknown to a single extrabiblical character in the whole vast literature of the ancient Near East.[8]

3. *Transition from Jacob to Joseph* (Gen. 34-36, 38)

The story of the rape of Dinah, the daughter of Jacob and Leah (34), is placed in Shechem, in the central hill country of Canaan where Jacob has moved sometime, apparently, after escaping Esau's invitation to settle beside him in Seir (see 33:17 ff.). Remembering Abraham's outright purchase of land for a family sepulcher near or in Mamre (Hebron) in the southern hill country (23), we see a further partial validation of Israel's claim to the land in the notice that Jacob also buys land in or near the city of Shechem (33:19).

In the past it has been common to give the story of Dinah —and indeed many other patriarchal narratives—a tribal interpretation. Shechem is a city inhabited by the tribe of Hamor. Dinah is a weak tribe aggressively assaulted by the tribe of Hamor. In this interpretation Simeon and Levi are also tribes, of course, who, in alliance with Dinah, wreak revenge upon the Hamorites in Shechem. This interpretation concludes the episode by seeing allusion to a final retaliation by Canaanites upon Simeon and Levi in the Blessing of Jacob:

> Cursed be their anger [Simeon and Levi], for it
>   is fierce;
>   and their wrath, for it is cruel!
> I will divide them in Jacob
>   and scatter them in Israel.
>
>   [49:7]

This is certainly ingenious, as is the similar interpretation of the death of Rachel at the birth of Benjamin (35:16 ff.), a story allegedly signifying the breakup of the Rachel tribe in Palestine when the tribe of Benjamin was formed after the acquisition of the land under Joshua.

But all of this is, to say the least, highly conjectural. Tribal implications there may be and no doubt are, and in the Dinah episode it may well be that characteristics of the tribes of Simeon and Levi are read into the men. There is a mutual relationship and agreement between Jacob's strongly-worded rebuke of the treacherous action of the two men (34:25-31)

and the pertinent words from the Blessing of Jacob, which
clearly reflects a postsettlement, and tribal, point of view:

> Simeon and Levi are brothers;
>> weapons of violence are their swords.
> O my soul, come not into their council;
>> O my spirit, be not joined to their company;
> for in their anger they slay men. . . .
>
> [49:5 f.]

But the admittedly neat package of the tribal interpretation is a little too neat; and it does violence to the vividness
and sense of reality which pervade the account of Gen. 34.
No less than other stories in the Jacob cycle, it reflects the
background of the patriarchal age—frictions between groups
(Hamor and Jacob); a level of sexual morality beyond the
reach of our judgment and in any judgment ennobled by
the integrity of Hamor and the love of his son for Dinah;
the effort on the part of both families to effect a peaceful
settlement honoring the religious sensibilities of the abused;
the despicable violation of the terms of agreement by two
of Jacob's sons; and finally, in perfect consonance with the
general character of Jacob, his sharp rebuke of his sons not
on moral but on utilitarian grounds:

> You have brought trouble on me by making me odious to the
> inhabitants of the land . . . my numbers are few, and if they
> gather themselves against me and attack me, I shall be destroyed,
> both I and my household.
>
> [34:30]

Jacob was not destroyed. But if we accept the present
sequence, he is apparently forced to move from Shechem to
Bethel, quite possibly a contributing factor in his loss of
Rachel at the birth of Benjamin. We see again in this narrative of chapter 35 the influence of faith upon the patriarchal

story. It is an age which accepts a corporate sense of responsibility: the guilt (or the merit—see the story of Abraham's intercession for Sodom and Gomorrah in ch. 14) of one or a few falls upon the entire family or the entire tribe or even, as we shall later see, upon the whole nation. Jacob-Israel, corporately, bears the responsibility for the treachery of Simeon and Levi. But again, and even with the possible implication of divine judgment in the death of Rachel, we see the repeated motif of the Jacob cycle: the tension between sin and divine grace, the expression of faith that Jacob-Israel is saved and redeemed only by the will and purpose of God (35:5), and finally the repetition of the promise and the blessing, and the second account of the changing of Jacob's name to Israel. In the concluding sequence (chs. 34-35) the essential structure of the Jacob narrative is reiterated.

Following the brief notice of Jacob's reunion with his father and brother and the death of Isaac (35:27-29) at Hebron in the south of Canaan, we read in chapter 36 a detailed Edomite genealogy, an extensive listing of the descendants of Esau. Apparently drawn from an old and reliable source, it includes the description of a division of land between Jacob and Esau strikingly similar to the more elaborate account of the separation of Abraham and Lot (36:6-8, cf. 13:5-12). The motive in the preservation of such stories is clear. Israel sees the legitimacy of her claim to the land not alone in the promise and gift of Yahweh. In the sustained if intermittent violent disputes with her near neighbors, Ammon and Moab (Lot), and Edom (Esau), Israel continues to recognize her close kinship with these semitic groups but insists in the stories that her claim to Canaan was validated long before she came out of Egypt and into the land under Joshua.

Finally, before turning to the Joseph story which begins

in chapter 37, we ought to look briefly at its abrupt inter-ruption in the narrative of chapter 38. It is clearly no part of the well-articulated and highly integrated narrative of Joseph. We can only guess as to why it stands where it does, why it came to its present position in Genesis. Perhaps this story of Judah and Tamar in chapter 38 is deliberately juxtaposed with the episode of Joseph's morally victorious encounter with his master's wife in Egypt in chapter 39 to point up the contrast between *a* son of Jacob and, at least for the remainder of Genesis, *the* son of Jacob. The same sharp contrast is an emphatic motif of the Tale of Joseph.

Whatever the reason for the insertion of chapter 38, it reflects in its present form an historical perspective later than the time of the great King David, about 1000 B.C. The story of Tamar and Judah is concerned with the genealogy of David: a product of this peculiar union is Perez who, accord-ing to the last verses of the book of Ruth (4:18-22), is an ancestor of David. We note also that the story illustrates a principle in Israel known as levirate marriage, and given legal formulation in Deuteronomy:

If brothers dwell together, and one of them dies and has no son, the wife of the dead shall not be married outside the family to a stranger; her husband's brother shall go in to her, and take her as his wife, and perform the duty of a husband's brother to her.

[Deut. 25:5]

Our story of Judah and his daughter-in-law Tamar, as also in fact the book of Ruth, indicates that in early Israel the levirate obligation might be extended to any near male rela-tive.[9] We note finally that this is a good story, not, obviously, in the sense that it is morally elevating (it candidly reflects the morality of the age), but in the remarkably graphic portrayal of character, especially Tamar, the deft integration of plot, and the skillful employment of suspense.

D. The Joseph Story (Gen. 37, 39-50)

1. *As Literature*

The Joseph narrative differs in marked degree from the cycles of stories about Abraham and Jacob. If the Jacob narratives appear to be somewhat better knit than the more episodic Abraham cycle, it is nevertheless clear that neither one has the integration of the Tale of Joseph. Here it is clearly *one* story, not a series of episodes. The plot is carefully, almost flawlessly, executed. There is no significant deviation from a central interest in the life and fortune of Joseph himself. The story moves, in highly integrated progression, from beginning to the high tension of its climax and finally to the moving resolution of the plot.

All the more remarkable, then—and all the more difficult of conclusive explanation—is the apparent phenomenon of a double tradition now unified in the single story. The usual explanation is that the present form of the narrative is a combination of J and E; and it is common to illustrate the alleged interweaving of the two accounts in an analysis of the first chapter in the tale, chapter 37. We are told that discrepancies in the chapter—such discrepancies certainly exist, here and elsewhere—are to be explained as follows. The two accounts, J and E, both draw from a common oral source, or, still as oral tradition, the Joseph story circulated simultaneously in central and southern Canaan. When given written form, the J version represented the peculiarities of the southern story, E, those of the northern account. The present form of the story is a skillful editorial combination of the two, designated JE.

Thus, according to J, it is *Judah* (with tribal residence in the south) who prevents the murder of Joseph and persuades his brothers instead to sell Joseph (vv. 26 and 27) to a passing band of *Ishmaelites* (v. 28b). But in the story according to E, it is *Reuben* (identified with the tribes settling through central Canaan) who interposes with advice that Joseph be placed in a pit—probably a well gone dry, or nearly dry—(vv. 22-24), from which predicament Joseph is extricated by passing *Midianites*. So, too, we are to explain other inconsistencies. The hate of the brothers is inspired by Joseph's tattling propensities and the favoritism of the father Jacob according to J (vv. 2-4, in part); while in E it is his obnoxious communication of his grandiose dreams to his brothers (vv. 5-11).

The hypothesis remains attractive. It also remains a hypothesis. But whether in fact the variants in the story are due to a written compilation from two parallel written accounts, or whether, as has been suggested of late, they are better attributed to natural deviations within a single oral tradition, we cannot now know. Acknowledging the variants, we find them hardly at all disruptive of the smooth flow and integration of the tale.

It is not surprising that the story of Joseph has inspired a distinguished literary work by one of the great novelists of modern time, the four Joseph novels by Thomas Mann. If his interpretations are not always our own, there are scenes and episodes which the reader of the Tetralogy will never forget: the inspired Tamar (38) motivated not by the simple passion of seduction but, convinced that Judah will bear the Blessing (see 49:8 ff.), by a profound determination to have a part in covenant history; or Serah, a granddaughter of Jacob, gracefully breaking the news of Joseph's survival to the old Patriarch in a song; or Mann's sensitive interpretation of the barrenness of Rachel as divine judgment not against Rachel herself, but against Jacob for his consuming and therefore idolatrous love of Rachel. But if one supposes that the moving subtleties of the Joseph novels are all Mann's creation, let him read the biblical story again![10]

2. *As History*

Genesis is an introduction to the story of Israel and as such it is clearly motivated in part by a concern to explain how and why that story has its historical beginning in Egypt. We have every reason to suspect that qualities inherent in folklore and legend have attached themselves to the person of Joseph, who provides the immediate link with Egypt. We quite agree that this is no more sober history than the narratives about Abraham, Isaac and Jacob. We, too, observe the fabulous fortunes of Joseph and understand the fictitious charge that Horatio Alger stole his plots from the story of Joseph. We also know that the Pharaoh of Egypt is nowhere named and that other details of the story suggest an imprecise contact with reality.

On the other hand, and surveying the total picture from Abraham to Joseph, we must also reaffirm the positive. If there is an imprecision in detail, the broad tones and the basic outlines convey a remarkably solid contact with reality. True, we still cannot even fix a date for Abraham, Jacob or Joseph. But we can say, on the strength of extrabiblical and *contemporary* archaeological evidence from Egypt north and east and south again around that fertile crescent, that Gen. 12-50 properly belongs to and is a part of the life of the ancient Near East during the first half of the second millennium B.C.

More particularly, and with pointed significance for the tale of Joseph, we know that Egypt, which earlier in this period controlled the affairs of Palestine, was itself under the rule of foreign dynasties (the fifteenth to the seventeenth dynasties) from a point in the eighteenth century to about the middle of the sixteenth century B.C. These conquerors of Egypt, known as the Hyksos, were, like the Hebrews, of Semitic stock; and although Egyptian records from the period are almost entirely lacking, a noted archaeologist and scholar is able to conclude on the evidence of records both before and after the period of Hyksos rule that "an intimate connection between the Hebrew settlement in Egypt and the Hyksos conquest may be considered certain."[11]

Under the circumstances of Semitic rule in Egypt, the story of the rise to power of a young and able Palestinian Semite is not at all in itself incredible. Nor, in view of the known influx into Egypt of large numbers of emigrants from Palestine and Syria during the Hyksos period, is it difficult to understand the residential move of the Jacob group (Gen. 47).

We do not want to overstate the measure of correlation between biblical story and external fact. On the other hand, it is important to recognize the general relationship between Gen. 12-50 and the actual life and times of the Patriarchal age. It is especially important for Old Testament study because, as almost every page of the Old Testament testifies, this correlation was deemed by Israel herself to be of prime importance! Against the charge that the faith of Israel always distorts the history of Israel, which, granted, it sometimes does, we have also to remember an integrity already given in the equation. It is a distinguishing characteristic of the faith of Israel from her earliest beginnings that God makes himself known in *history*, that is, in the course of human events. God, this Yahweh, is the be-all and end-all of Israel's existence; and if that *summum bonum* of the knowledge of

God is to be had, it must be had in the knowledge of what takes place in the human arena of history. In such a faith, Israel will not knowingly and willfully distort the image of history in which alone she can find the image of God.

And so, we call it legend. Perhaps there is no better term to convey at once both a measurable and significant correlation with external reality on the one hand, and, on the other, an imprecision in sequence and detail. And yet we find ourselves in the strongest agreement with the German scholar, Professor von Rad, whom we have cited before, in his own expressed feeling that after all, legend is not an adequate term, so long as it is commonly understood simply as a mixture of history and unrestrained popular imagination (one part history, nine parts imagination—our comment, not his). We much better understand legend as a combination of history and meditation, and as motivated primarily by a concern to give expression to the meaning of history, as that meaning is conveyed by the faith that God makes himself known therein.[12]

3. As Faith

There are differences of a literary kind between the narratives of Joseph and Abraham-Jacob. There is also the strong suggestion of a somewhat different theological perspective underlying these narratives. We sense in the Joseph story in contrast to the Abraham-Jacob cycles what we may call for want of a better term a theological sophistication. Yahweh demands of Joseph no sacrifice (Abraham–22). There is no face-to-face-ness (18) and certainly no wrestling with the deity (Jacob–32). There is no tension in Joseph himself between faith and unfaith (Abraham), or between his own sinfulness and the grace of God (Jacob). Rather, insofar as these tensions appear, it is Joseph's brothers who reflect them. It is they, the sons of Jacob, the children of Israel, who violate the covenant faith, who act in ignorance or defiance of the divine promise, who take matters of the covenant family into their own hands and act in unfaith. It is their own evil intention, their sinfulness—not Joseph's—that is forgiven. It is they who are divinely judged in the precariousness of their own existence. It is they who are redeemed by the grace and mercy of God *in spite of* their evil intention. All of this is given summary expression in Joseph's words to his brothers at the scene of their final reconciliation:

As for you, you meant evil against me; but God meant it for good. . . .

[50:20]

No less than in the Abraham and Jacob stories, Israel reads in the Joseph story something of her own inner experience of life lived under the rule and covenant of God. But the continuity of analogy is in the brothers not Joseph.

What, then, of Joseph? What is Joseph's place in the faith of Israel? How does the character of Joseph reflect the faith of Israel? And if the characterization is in part shaped by faith, what is its message back to the community of faith out of which it grew and in which it was cherished?

We do not pretend to be in a position to give a final answer to these questions; and in attempting answers, we are aware of other questions inherent in the very answers. We have already suggested a particular correspondence between Abraham and Jacob and the first and second phases of Israel's history, respectively. We have tried to show, to be sure briefly, that the Abraham cycle is particularly relevant in the faith of Israel to that first historical epoch in Israel's history when she left a land (Egypt) to gain a land (Canaan);

while the same is to be said of the Jacob cycle and its relatedness in faith to the story of Israel *in* the land of promise.

We wonder if there does not exist a comparable relationship of correspondence between the Joseph story and that third phase of Israel's history which is separated from the second by the sixth-century catastrophe of the Fall of the state of Israel and the Babylonian Exile. The prophets of Israel, many of them standing between the glorious event of the Exodus and the tragic event of the Fall, interpreted both events as essentially the same in character, that is, as resulting from the purposive action of God in history. They predicted the Fall, or saw it in retrospect, as the judgment of God upon an unfaithful and sinful nation, but they understood the function of the catastrophe to be ultimately, like the Exodus event, positive and redemptive in character. The covenant, violated by Israel, was *God's* covenant, and the judgment, so far from terminating the covenant, was seen as the only means of effectively perpetuating the covenant purpose—now in a purified *remnant* of the nation, or in *one* from the nation. The remnant or the one, and we find both concepts before as well as after the Fall, is a projection of faith, an assertion of hope in the ultimate fulfillment of the covenant promise. What we term Messianism is essentially this faith, this hope. The word Messiah, which means literally "anointed one," points strictly, of course, to an individual; but in the psychology of Israel with its facile and often unconscious transitions from individual to corporate personality, we are hardly wrong in allowing a broader definition to the term Messianism, in which emphasis is placed upon the redemptive *function* of the human entity, whether group or individual. We are only lately coming to understand this characteristic psychological relationship between the one and the many in Israel; but it is with this understanding that we may see Messianism in the broadest sense in the divine promise to Abraham: "In you all the families of the earth will be blessed" (12:3, R.S.V. margin).

We wonder whether we do not have also to interpret the Joseph story in the same broad sense of Messianism, and as expecially corresponding to that third phase of Israel's life in which the messianic hope came into sharpest focus. Joseph is one of the sons of Jacob, to be sure; but he is much more one *from* the children of Israel. His uniqueness, his separation, is a theme of the Genesis narratives long before the notice of his birth (30:24) in the repeated accent through the Jacob cycle on the notes of Jacob's consuming love and the barrenness of Rachel. And if the introductory chapter in the Joseph story (37) is in fact a combination of J and E, we see again the "method in the madness" that wove them together in the consequently doubled emphasis on the separation of Joseph from the group: it is Joseph against, and therefore set off from, his brothers in bringing the ill report (37:2, E); it is Joseph whom "Israel loved . . . more than any other of his children" (v. 3, J); the "robe with sleeves" (R.S.V.; robe of many colors in some of the older translations) is given to Joseph (v. 3b, E); and it is Joseph who dreams the dreams of his own uniqueness (vv. 5 ff., E).

Joseph is not so much one *of* the brothers as he is one *from* the brothers. His very survival (how strongly suggestive of the nation's Fall and Restoration) is from the human standpoint incredible, to say nothing of the final position of power which he attains. Against fantastic human odds, God preserves the life of Joseph and brings him at length to that position in which he is responsible for saving the life not only of the Jacob-Israel group, but indeed of the whole world:

Moreover, *all the earth* came to Egypt *to Joseph* to buy grain, because the famine was severe over all the earth.

[41:57]

The same motif of salvation is expressed in spiritualized terms by a great anonymous prophet who, in the time not long after the fall of the state of Israel, sees the means of salvation emerging in the Servant of Yahweh. The Servant may be one, or, collectively, many, but this entity embodies the ultimate fulfillment of Israel's covenant hope:

> It is too light a thing that you should be my
> servant
> to raise up the tribes of Jacob
> and to restore the preserved of Israel;
> I will give you as a light to the nations,
> that my salvation may reach to the end of
> the earth.
>
> [Isa. 49:6]

If there is a particular correspondence in Abraham to the first Israel (Exodus and Settlement) and in Jacob to the second (the period of the Kingdoms), something of the same correspondence is to be seen in Joseph to the third Israel, to her profound hope that out of willful intention of evil, out of the consequent judgment of destruction and tragedy, God would yet through human means raise up the tribes of Jacob and bring his light of redemption to all the earth.

The correspondence, as with Abraham and Jacob, is imprecise. In the Joseph story too the players speak their own lines, lines created long before the historical phases to which they bear their correspondence. We do not for a moment mean to suggest that Gen. 12-50 was created out of whole cloth as an allegorical, fictional, personalized "history" of Israel. On the contrary, we have tried to make it plain that the bulk of the material comes *in fact* out of Israel's ancient past, transmitted first orally, and given its most significant written formulation by the Yahwist in the tenth century B.C., when the second phase of Israel's history was only just beginning to unfold. Nor do we mean to say, then, that the story of Joseph came into being as a messianic message with the intention of treating Joseph as a messianic figure. We do mean to suggest the possibility and even the probability that in the unmistakable implications of messianism in Joseph, the *germ* of the later development of the concept was something already *given* in Israel's early traditions, precisely as the germinal faith in one God as Creator (Gen. 2), Judge (3-11) and Redeemer (12 ff.) was also given in the same traditions received by the Yahwist.

These concepts certainly underwent development and elaboration in the course of Israel's literary history, and beyond any doubt the meaning and significance of these given qualities of faith and hope came to full realization in Israel only as her history moved from high promise to frustration and finally to the rebirth of hope. Nor do *we*, at least, doubt that the unfolding meaning of all that was given in early tradition was in appreciable measure reflected in the long editorial process of the compilation of the present Old Testament canon. And here we must speak with real appreciation for the hypothesis of documents underlying the present text. Whatever the literal accuracy of the scheme of JEDP (in Genesis JEP), the fact of periodic and thorough rethinking and rearrangement of the material is indisputable: the scheme of documents at least reflects the certainty that the tradition maintained a strong vitality and relevance in the life of Israel throughout Old Testament history. If what is conveyed in the sequence of symbols J–E–JE–P–JEP (by R = Redactor)—and we are thinking only of Genesis now— be sometime proved in error, the symbolism nevertheless testifies with essential accuracy to the continuing discovery in every age of Israel's history of the fresh import and meaning of what was already given in her earliest traditions.

Finally, then, Genesis receives its last rethinking, its ultimate refinement in the age of restoration following Israel's destruction and exile. The last edition of Genesis is the work of an editor, a redactor who surveys the full sweep of Israel's history. We call him R; and in his case, too, we cannot be sure whether he was one or many. It does not matter. Nor do we know the extent of his revision. It was probably very slight, beyond the work of combining earlier works. But as the Yahwist had done centuries earlier, he left behind him not only an introduction to the history of Israel, but a theological prelude sounding now the themes recurrent and dominant in the history which he surveyed.

It is in this sense that we may say of Genesis that it both informs and is informed by that which it introduces. It is in this sense that we may speak of Genesis as a "meditation on history."[13] Gerhard von Rad recalls with approval the suggestion of the Jewish biblical scholar Franz Rosenzweig: we ought no longer to think of the symbol R as standing for Redactor but rather, for *Rabbenu,* which means, in Hebrew, "our master"; since for the final form in which we receive the work, we are indebted to him and to his interpretation.[14] His was the same historical perspective which gave rise to this prayer:

Thou art the Lord, the God who didst choose Abram and bring him forth . . . and give him the name Abraham; and thou didst find his heart faithful before thee, and didst make with him the covenant. . . .

[Neh. 9:7 f.]

III. HISTORY

The King Walks before You: I Sam. 12–I Kings 11

We shall not elaborate evidence of a double or multiple source tradition underlying Samuel and Kings. Inconsistencies in fact and point of view and the duplication of episodes are apparent even to the casual reader; and detailed analysis of the text is easily accessible in any standard Introduction to the Old Testament.[1] We are skeptical of some of the common criteria of literary priority, however; and we reject the view that the "later" sources (often late only editorially, not in substance) are necessarily less accurate, less dependable. If the "later" sources are interpretative, as they are, *so are the earlier*. We do not think there is anywhere in the Bible a purely objective, detached account of sequential events. *If* we have such an account anywhere in the Old Testament, it is II Sam. 9-20; but even here we are given an interpretation of human events through the eyes of profound faith. We have also to remember what we have emphasized before, that the later "documents" used in the compilation of the Pentateuch and the historical writings have obviously made use of older and, on the whole, factually reliable sources.

Early and late, Israel's historians are better understood in Aristotle's definition of a poet. Aristotle's historian was a mere chronicler of sequential events; his poet was one who distilled from the chronological catalogue its essence, its universal judgment and meaning.[2] This is not to say that the

writers of history in Israel are unconcerned with matters of
fact. They are profoundly concerned with the visible structure of the event precisely because they regard the ultimate
function of historical writing to be the communication of
meaning in history. If absolute precision in detail is of
secondary importance, the essential structure of what in
fact occurred is crucial because the meaning is always in
terms of divine nature, divine will and divine intention. The
essence of history, which must of course be extracted from
the *actual* event, is the revelation, the self-disclosure, of God.

What we term earlier and later sources do sometimes differ in detail; but we suspect that they differ in the representation of a given event not always because they were compiled in different centuries, but because the two sources
reflect opposing *contemporaneous* interpretations. For example, we think it reasonable to suppose that the establishment of the monarchy was viewed, *at the time*,[3] in the two
different and opposing interpretations now combined in
I Samuel. Many in Israel, perhaps most, looked on the
innovation favorably, as reflected in the "A" or earlier source;
but we do not doubt that even at the time the step was
regarded with disapproval among conservative Yahweh
loyalists. Certainly some of these regarded the monarchy as
an affront to Yahweh and as an easy road to apostasy, and
this is the point of view of the later "B" source. Israel's
historians who stand further from the event will of course
use the records at their disposal in such a way as to emphasize
their own disillusionment with a monarchy that has failed to
realize the high hopes of its founding; but we are hardly
therefore justified in dismissing the B source as inaccurate or
unhistorical. And in any interpretation of Old Testament
history compiled from a plurality of sources, it is important
to recognize the essential unity commonly underlying differ-

ences in representation of both detail and point of view. Old Testament history is always understood as history in which (1) Yahweh acts (2) toward the fulfillment of his own purposes. Thus, the two conflicting narrative strands both understand that the institution of monarchy results at Yahweh's instigation, through the instrumentality of Samuel. This is no less true of B (see I Sam. 8:4-9) than of A (I Sam. 9:15 ff.).

We are therefore unwilling always and automatically to accord higher historical validity to the "older" source, or superiority of interpretation to the "prior" source. In modern as well as ancient times we understand history to be more than the accurate record of event. It is also the interpretation of the event, an interpretation to be sure requiring knowledge of the contemporary understanding of the event, but never complete until set in the perspective which only time can give. We must record and interpret the Stalin-Roosevelt-Churchill era knowing not only the limitations of the interpretation but indeed of the record itself! Both the record and the interpretation will ultimately be determined by future generations of historians and writers. The essence which we extract, the meaning which we read, may or may not be theirs; but the history of this era remains incomplete until it is rerecorded and reinterpreted in the perspective of the future. And this is to speak of the wholeness of history, as true of ancient history as it is of modern history. The Old Testament possesses this wholeness in marked degree, and to devaluate the later material is to prefer a partial history, and even a distorted history, to a whole history.

And Samuel said to all Israel, ". . . behold, the king walks before you; and I am old and gray . . . stand still, that I may plead with you before the Lord concerning all the saving deeds of the Lord which he performed for you and for your fathers. When Jacob went into Egypt. . . .

[I Sam. 12:2, 7 f.]

The speech that follows, placed upon the lips of Samuel as a farewell address, suggests some kinship in point of view with that which characterizes much of the book of Deuteronomy. In its present form substantially from the seventh century but embodying older material, Deuteronomy proclaims an absolute correlation between the faithfulness of Israel and her national security. So does the speech before us in I Sam. 12:

If you will fear the Lord and serve him and hearken to his voice and not rebel against the commandment of the Lord, . . . it will be well; but if you will not. . . .

[12:14 f.]

Do we therefore conclude that the speech actually dates from the seventh century? Possibly—in its present form. But the content of the historical summary, if not the form (vv. 8-13), has the ring of authentic antiquity and may well have been drawn from a source similar to the cultic credos which we find in Deut. 26:5-9, 6:20-24 and Josh. 24:2-13.[4]

In any case, editorial design here conforms to a consistent pattern, a pattern which reflects the faith of the community of Israel: at every decisive transition in her recorded history she hears from the lips of the preceding period's most influential figure a summary of her past precisely in terms of "the saving deeds of the Lord." We are, she affirms repeatedly, where we are and what we are because of what Yahweh has done. This is the import and function of the postexilic prayer of Ezra (Neh. 9), in which the long centuries are remembered and interpreted as God's activity in history. But several centuries earlier, Israel reads the whole book of

Deuteronomy with its repeated emphasis upon what God has done as "the words that Moses spoke to all Israel" (Deut. 1:1) at the close of his life. And similarly, when possession is taken of the land and Joshua's work is done, we read as if from his lips that magnificent confessional recital of past events in Josh. 24:2 ff.

So, in transition from tribal confederation to monarchy, Israel appropriately hears on the lips of Samuel a summary of the past as essentially the story of "the saving deeds of the Lord."

A. SAUL (I SAM. 13-15)

We do not know the length of Saul's reign. As the Revised Standard Version indicates in I Sam. 13:1, two crucial facts are missing—Saul's age when he began to reign, and the duration of his reign. Nor can we fix exactly his dates in history. We may guess that he reigned for not less than twenty years, and that he died about 1000 B.C.

In the brief section now under discussion, little comment is needed on chapter 14. Israel, outnumbered and out-equipped by the Philistines, wins a victory made possible by the personal courage, daring and combat skill of Saul's son Jonathan and his loyal aide (14:7). It is an account which richly informs us of the mind and temper of the age. We note especially Saul's ban upon eating (v. 24); Jonathan's innocent violation of the prohibition and his remarkable protest against its woeful inexpediency (vv. 27 ff.); Saul's religious scruples in his insistence that the sacrificial procedure be properly carried out; his apparent assumption of the role of priest (vv. 31-35); the clear indication of the nature of the Urim and Thummim as sacred lots cast to determine divine will (v. 41); and finally, the incidental insight we are given into the profoundly democratic nature of Israel's early monarchy in the effective popular protest to Saul's sentence of death upon Jonathan (vv. 43-45).

Chapters 13 and 15 may best be considered together because the two stories say essentially the same thing. In both, Israel is interpreting the reign of Saul: Saul transgresses the commandment of God, made known through Samuel, and is divinely judged, again through Samuel, with loss of the kingship.

The two stories concern different events, to be sure. In chapter 13 (as in 14:31 ff.), Saul takes upon himself the priestly function of Samuel (vv. 11 and 12). In chapter 15, he violates the explicit commandment of Samuel, which is tantamount to the commandment of Yahweh: he fails to observe the ancient practice known among the Hebrews as the *herem*, by which the defeated enemy is *totally* destroyed on the spot as an act of devotion to the deity. The fact that this is in our eyes an appallingly brutal concept is irrelevant to our understanding of Israel's interpretation of the event. This is Israel under Saul in the eleventh century B.C., not the Western nations of the twentieth century A.D. At a later time Israel herself would have repudiated the practice. But Saul, a child of his own age, believed with Samuel and with ancient Israel that the *herem* was the will of God.

We may add here, therefore, parenthetically, that whatever else we may mean when we speak of inspiration and revelation in the Old Testament, we certainly do not mean any radical or miraculous emancipation from the general mores, perspectives and knowledge of the age. The vitality of the Old Testament literature and the vigorous communication of its faith are primarily due to the intimacy of its relationship to historical reality.

The circumstances of the two stories in I Sam. 13 and 15 differ, but they express the same understanding of Saul's reign. Israel reads and records history, as it does myth and legend, through the eyes of faith. Saul's failure to establish himself and his descendants at the head of the monarchy is due to his disobedience and the consequent divine judgment upon it. In these two narratives, we have the turning point of Saul's reign. In the covenant community he has violated the terms of kingship—obedience to Yahweh. The judgment is expulsion. To be sure, Saul continues in nominal rule until his death; but from this point on in the records of his reign he not only is in process of losing the kingdom, but stands in tragic awareness that it is already lost (see, e.g., I Sam. 23:17).

We cannot know to what degree Israel identifies her own life with that of the king. Certainly she sees herself and all men in the story of the Garden (Gen. 2-3), which is strikingly similar in structure to the story of Saul. A comparison of the two stories will give us a better understanding of Israel's interpretation of the reign of Saul. The correspondence is due, of course, not to any conscious literary dependence of one narrative upon the other, but to a consistent and unifying quality of faith in Israel: human sin and divine judgment are regarded as fundamental and formative realities in experience and history.

It is Yahweh who places man in the garden and Saul in the kingdom—both under the most propitious circumstances. The one condition that both must observe is obedience to Yahweh. But this condition is willfully violated by both, and on the same grounds—the *reasonableness* of the disobedient act. There is even an effort on the part of both man and king to shift the blame to someone else. After Samuel's brilliant retort to Saul's overeager, guilt-betraying protest of obedience (I Sam. 15:13-14), and his indictment of the king, Saul attempts at once to clear himself and to justify his action:

... I have utterly destroyed the Amalekites. But the *people* took of the spoil, sheep and oxen, the best of the things devoted to destruction, *to sacrifice to the Lord your God in Gilgal.*

[See vv. 21-22; cf. 13:11 f.]

In just the same way is man's disobedience in the garden rationalized:

So when the woman saw that the tree was good for food, and that it was a delight to the eyes, and that the tree was to be desired to make one wise, she took of its fruit and ate; and she gave some to her husband, and he ate.

[Gen. 3:6]

And when he is indicted, man too attempts to shift the blame:

The woman whom thou gavest to be with me, she gave me fruit of the tree, and I ate.

[Gen. 3:12]

Samuel's answer to Saul, coming as it does in a context of eleventh-century superstition and brutality (the *herem*), is all the more to be appreciated as a shaft of clear inspiration. Despite the particular comparative (sacrifice) employed, Samuel enunciates a central quality of the faith of Israel that is also implicit in the story of the garden: the universal condition of life is obedience of God. Certainly Samuel's specific words are not only addressed to the king but to all Israel:

To obey is better than sacrifice
and to hearken than the fat of rams.
[I Sam. 15:22b]

The comparison between man in the Garden and Saul in the kingdom does not stop here. In both narratives, when the condition of tenure is violated, appropriate judgment is announced and executed. The judgment is expulsion! It might be argued from the analogy of Gen. 2-3 that in the faith of Israel the sin of Saul is essentially the sin of all men. In any case, Israel knew in the story of Saul her own disobedience; and she came to know in the sixth century the same judgment upon it—the expulsion of the Exile.

It will become apparent as we move on in the narratives of Saul and David that we cannot but regard Saul with sympathy. He stands as a profoundly tragic figure on the pages of Israel's history. His public life begins with the highest promise. He possesses the physical and moral attributes of a king—physique, initiative and courage. He is elevated to prominence as a result of a combination of personal qualities, all contributing to his stature as a leader (I Sam. 11). Among these, we note what has been called the "charismatic" quality which the historical narratives refer to in this way: "And the spirit of God came mightily upon Saul . . ." (11:6). We remember these attributes. But we remember, too, the odds against him—the critically low ebb of the life of the Israelite confederacy; the steady depletion of life and goods under the incessant raids of neighboring states to the east and south; and the multiple group and tribal loyalties offering obstinate resistance against efforts toward unity. And always there were the Philistines! Here is an eloquent description of Israel's impotence under Philistine domination:

Now there was no smith to be found throughout all the land of Israel; for the Philistines said, "Lest the Hebrews make themselves swords or spears"; but every one of the Israelites went down to the Philistines to sharpen his plowshare, his mattock, his axe, or his sickle. . . . So on the day of the battle there was neither sword nor spear found in the hand of any of the people with Saul and Jonathan. . . .

[I Sam. 13:19, 20, 22]

We speak of odds: Saul not only begins without army—he began without weapons!

Even a highly endowed personality like Saul's could hardly hold out against such odds, and under such tensions. The remainder of Saul's life as king is one of increasing emotional agony, plagued with a steadily advancing sickness of spirit and a deepening sense of persecution at the hands not only of subjects and friends, but even of daughter and son.

We remember, too, that in some quarters in Israel that tragic life continued to command respect. David, Saul's successor, consistently refused to violate either the person or the office of Saul and composed at his death a deeply moving lament (II Sam. 1:19-27). And one of Israel's historians records this estimate of Saul's accomplishments:

> When Saul had taken the kingship over Israel, he fought against all his enemies on every side. . . . And he did valiantly . . . and delivered Israel out of the hands of those who plundered them.
>
> [I Sam. 14:47 f.]

B. SAUL AND DAVID (I SAM. 16–II SAM. 8)

It is obvious that Samuel's farewell address in I Sam. 12 is somewhat premature. Saul's failure to observe the *herem* in chapter 15 is corrected in person by the prophet-priest Samuel "before the Lord in Gilgal" (15:32 ff.). The gruesome details hardly suggest an old man on the brink of the grave. And now Samuel, who has been Yahweh's instrument in making one king, proceeds at once with the making of another (16:1-13).

We find it difficult to accept at face value all the details of the narratives about Samuel. We observe an abnormally wide range in character. In the most primitive representation Samuel is a "seer" possessing and exercising on a fee basis certain occult powers (so, in the main, I Sam. 9:1-10:16, and ch. 11 from the earliest, or A, source). But he is also repeatedly cast directly or inferentially in the role of priest; or stress is placed upon his function as a prophet (in the sense, simply, of a spokesman for Yahweh; so, e.g., ch. 15); or he is represented as the Judge of all Israel (so, e.g., 8, 10:17-27, and ch. 12, in the main from a later, or B, source). These later narrative strands have tended to "modernize" Samuel's role as prophet and seventh-century Deuteronomic editing has doubtless idealized his function as judge. On the other hand, we see little reason to doubt that Samuel did exercise a multiple function in Israel; that he did in fact combine in himself certain qualities of seer, priest, prophet and judge, consistent, to be sure, with his age and time; and that he performed substantially as represented the function of king-maker in early Israel.

So now in a narrative placing heavy stress upon *Yahweh's* election, Yahweh's choice, David, the youngest son of Jesse, is anointed king by Samuel. As with Saul, the narrative imputes at once the "charismatic" quality to David, the free "gift," the "endowment" of the spirit of Yahweh:

Then Samuel took the horn of oil, and anointed him in the midst of his brothers; and the Spirit of the Lord came mightily upon David from that day forward.

[16:13]

If, as scholars in textual analysis believe, this narrative (16: 1-13) is from the B complex and that which follows (vv. 14-23) is a part of the A source, we must remark the editorial skill that combined them; for immediately we read:

Now the Spirit of the Lord departed from Saul, and an evil spirit from the Lord tormented him.

[16:14]

The *charisma* (a Greek term that literally means "gift" or "endowment") has passed from Saul to David! The memory of early Israel, standing very close to Saul, is preserved here. This contemporaneous or nearly contemporaneous view of the tragic king explains the phenomenon of his emotional instability in its own terms: the positive character of the younger Saul ("the Spirit of Yahweh . . . ," 11:6) is not now merely neutralized, it is negativized! The history states it very simply: "an evil spirit from Yahweh tormented him" (16:14b). And tragedy is compounded for Saul, although he does not yet know it, in this bitter irony: the man to whom the charismatic quality has been transferred, the one to whom the kingdom is to be given—this same son of Jesse alone has gifts to soothe Saul's tormented spirit. David is brought into the service of Saul—and (v. 22), "Saul loved him greatly."

And whenever the evil spirit from God was upon Saul, David took the lyre and played it with his hand; so Saul was refreshed, and was well, and the evil spirit departed from him.

[16:23]

If the young Saul was possessed of kingly attributes, Israel's historians would have us understand that David is the kingly man *par excellence*. The popular—and no doubt at points contemporary—estimate of David is repeated throughout the history:

Now he was ruddy, and had beautiful eyes, and was handsome.

[16:12]

[He is] skilful in playing, a man of valor, a man of war, prudent in speech, and a man of good presence; and the Lord is with him.

[16:18]

Saul has slain his thousands,
And David his ten thousands.
[18:7, 21:11, 29:5]

The words of Abigail addressed directly to David also reflect the popular estimate:

... my lord [David] is fighting the battles of Yahweh; and evil shall not be found in you so long as you live [but this, as we shall see, is extreme hyperbole!] ... the life of my lord shall be bound in the bundle of the living in the care of the Lord your God.

[I Sam. 25:28 f.]

... everything that the king did pleased all the people.

[II Sam. 3:36]

David administered justice and equity to all his people.

[II Sam. 8:15]

So, too, these two statements to David from the wise woman of Tekoa:

... my lord the king is like the angel of God to discern good and evil ... my lord has wisdom like the wisdom of the angel of God to know all things that are on the earth.

[II Sam. 14:17, 20]

Early and late in Israel, David is remembered as *the* king and the hopes of subsequent generations for the fulfillment of the covenant promises always tend to center in the *re*-establishment of the Davidic era under another David, a son of David, "a shoot from the stump of Jesse ... a branch ... out of his roots" (Isa. 11:1).

There is hardly a literate person in the Western world who does not know the outline of the story of David's conquest of the giant Philistine, Goliath (I Sam. 17). In its present form it is a relatively late narrative which duplicates (vv. 55-58) the episode of David's introduction to Saul already recounted under different circumstances in the preceding chapter. Furthermore, the actual feat of the slaughter of Goliath is attributed to one Elhanan in II Sam. 21:19.

And there was again war with the Philistines at Gob; and Elhanan, the son of Jaareoregim, the Bethlehemite, slew Goliath the Gittite, the shaft of whose spear was like a weaver's beam.

Whatever the explanation of the contradiction, it is remarkable that this notice remained in the text of the books of Samuel; and its very presence testifies to the integrity of the process of transmitting the text. As a general critical principle we must acknowledge the probability that the heroic deed was performed by the lesser man and subsequently transferred in tradition to the greater man. It is almost impossible to conceive of the transfer in reverse.

What, then, of the historicity of David's feat, if Elhanan, one of David's mighty warriors, and not David himself, slew "Goliath, of Gath [=the Gittite] . . . the shaft of [whose] spear was like a weaver's beam" (I Sam. 17:4, 7, in part)? It is clearly the same Philistine champion in both accounts, and we can hardly accept the effort of the writer of Chronicles to remove the contradiction as he does with an augmented sentence:

And there was again war with the Philistines; and Elhanan the son of Jair slew *Lahmi the brother of* Goliath the Gittite, the shaft . . . .

[I Chron. 20:5]

There is evidence that the story of I Sam. 17 may originally have been considerably shorter than in its present form. The Greek translation of the Old Testament, known as the Septuagint, and completed in the closing centuries of the pre-Christian era, omits vv. 17-31 and 55-59 in one of its best extant manuscripts. This removes not only the duplication of David's introduction to Saul (16:19 ff. and 17:55 ff.) but the discrepancy within chapter 17 between Saul and David's meeting before the fight with Goliath (vv. 32 ff.) and Saul's question to Abner after the slaying of Goliath, "whose son is this youth?" (v. 55). We can hardly accuse the Greek translators of deliberately curtailing the text for these reasons. It is much more probable that they translated exactly what they found in the Hebrew manuscript before them and that literary tradition had preserved a shorter and perhaps the original form of the story.

This leaves us, nevertheless, with the problem of Goliath. We think it is a problem which inheres in the name of the Philistine champion, not in the feat. David's performance of such an act of personal heroism is quite consistent with the general portrayal of the younger David: indeed, such a deed as this goes far in explaining the ease and speed with which he gained such prominence and popularity in Israel. But we are inclined to think that the Philistine giant named Goliath was in fact dispatched by Elhanan and not by David. If we are right in these assumptions, the best explanation is that only the *name* of Goliath is an essential error of the present story and that it is a later addition to the narrative in the *only* place where it appeared in the original story, namely, at 17:4. We are not, therefore, inclined to refute the substance of the story of David and Goliath, but only the name of David's antagonist.[5]

A new motif is now introduced, chapter 18, with startling abruptness—the love between Jonathan and David. These first five verses also appear to be from a later source (they are omitted too in the same manuscript of the Greek translation), but the information imparted, though premature and out of sequence, is certainly in essence true, as subsequent narratives testify.

Saul's jealousy takes form at once and in extreme degree, not only because of David's great popularity (18:7) but also because Saul recognizes that David now possesses the charismatic quality, the peculiar endowment of Yahweh which Saul himself had previously possessed.

> Saul was afraid of David, because the Lord was with him but had departed from Saul.
>
> [18:12]

Saul's torment appears to be a deep emotional illness. Twice he makes an attempt on David's life. Failing each time, and driven to further demonic measures by the love of Michal, his own daughter, for David, he sets what he hopes will be a fatal price on Michal's hand—the foreskins of a hundred Philistines. There is a note of brutal, ironic humor here. The Philistines did not, as the Israelites, practice circumcision and all Israel must have felt delight and a certain rough amusement in the feat of David and his men circumcising in death not merely a hundred, but two hundred, of the uncircumcised enemy! The chapter concludes, appropriately, with this notice:

> Saul gave him his daughter Michal for a wife. But when Saul saw and knew that the Lord was with David, and that all Israel loved him, Saul was still more afraid. So Saul was David's enemy continually.
>
> [18:28 ff.]

The relationship between Jonathan and David is introduced again in chapter 19, with Jonathan interceding with his father on David's behalf. We are given insight into the real sickness of Saul: here, and again later, Saul renounces his jealousy, only to be seized by it again, irresistibly. Again Saul makes an attempt on David's life, while David is playing before him. Again Saul follows up his person-to-person attempt with a carefully planned scheme, only to be foiled this time by the deception of his own daughter.

The account of David's taking refuge with Samuel at Naioth is intimately revealing of the psychological complexion of the religious beliefs and practices of the time, even though we are unable to explain the situation completely. This time Saul's efforts to take David are frustrated by a religious phenomenon known among the Canaanites and common in early Israel.

Saul sent messengers to take David; and when they saw the company of the prophets prophesying, and Samuel standing as head over them, the Spirit of God came upon the messengers of Saul, and they also prophesied.

[19:20]

Two sets of messengers, and finally Saul himself, undergo the same seizure, all in explanation, apparently, of a kind of proverb about Saul—"Is Saul also among the prophets?" (See the duplicate and differing explanation of the same proverb in I Sam. 10:10-12.)

This kind of ecstatic prophecy differs radically from that of the great prophets of Israel who appear later, from the eighth to the sixth centuries. What is described here is an observable psychic phenomenon, an uninhibited ecstasy that culminated, at least on occasion (as with Saul), in a state of trance. The seizure was induced by group participation, and was obviously contagious. Apparently both the participants and the observers explained the phenomenon as a temporary seizure by "the Spirit of God." Significantly, the word used for deity here is not Yahweh, a term peculiar to Israel, but the widespread general designation *elohim*. This seizure is not the same as the more permanent *endowment* with the Spirit of Yahweh, the charismatic gift, that Saul and David experienced. Rather, it is a momentary and sporadic "possession" by unseen powers, induced by primitive group dynamics, and expressed in ecstatic behavior. The same phenomenon is known to have existed among Israel's neighbors and it has persisted in the history of religion down to our own time, when, even in certain contemporary Christian sects, it may still be observed.

Now, chapter 20, David finds Jonathan:

What have I done? What is my guilt? And what is my sin before your father, that he seeks my life? . . . truly, as the Lord lives and as your soul lives, there is but a step between me and death.

[20:1, 3, in part]

This history offers an incomparable study in relationships —David and Jonathan, David and Saul, Saul and Jonathan. It is also a penetrating study of character. The narrative and the dialogue are marked by subtlety, and an exceedingly deft, though simple, appeal is made to the full range of emotional response. Saul, already a tragic figure, now suffers the anguish of alienation from his own son and David learns that if he is to live at all, he must live in exile.

In what follows we want merely to underline, as it were, certain points of the text. From I Sam. 20 through II Sam. 6 the narrative thread is coherent and, with the exception of I Sam. 24, the great bulk of the material is drawn, apparently, from the same early source.

Take special note of the following:

The portrayal of the despicable Doeg, the Edomite, chief of Saul's herdsmen (I Sam. 21-22).

The colorful four-verse episode of David before Achish, king of Gath, one of the five Philistine cities, with Achish's retort to his retinue in angry humor (21:12 ff.).

The nature and character of David's outlaw band (22:2).

David's cordial relationship with the kingdom of Moab (more often a bitter foe of Israel), and the sinister implications of his parents' refuge there (22:3 f.).

Saul, suffering now the ravages of a deep sense of persecution (22:6-8 and cf. 23:21 quoted below).

Saul's torment reflected in his unwarranted and unmerciful slaughter of the priests of Nob (22:11 ff.) ; the lone escape of Abiathar (v. 20 f.) ; David's profoundly sensitive, deeply revealing response to Abiathar; and the classical simplicity and dignity of the language:

> I knew on that day, when Doeg the Edomite was there, that he would surely tell Saul. I have occasioned the death of all the persons of your father's house. Stay with me, fear not; for he that seeks my life seeks your life; with me you shall be in safekeeping.
>
> [22:22 f.]

David's faithfulness to Yahweh, tinged perhaps with expediency, but devoted and uncompromised; the implicit reminder that the Spirit of Yahweh continued to rest upon David; and the historian's (and Israel's) conviction that David is perculiarly Yahweh's man (23:2, 8 ff., 14b) .

Jonathan's words to David, potently suggestive (1) of the now thoroughly desperate character of Saul's continuing jealousy and (2) of the total eclipse of any personal ambition in Jonathan by his love and admiration for David:

> Fear not; for the hand of Saul my father shall not find you; you shall be king over Israel, and I shall be next to you; Saul my father also knows this.
>
> [23:17]

Saul, now a pathetic figure, fighting a battle already lost in his own mind, persuaded that from the narrow circle of family out to the broad circle of the world, everyone is against him; seizing gratefully upon the offer of the Ziphites to surrender David to him:

> May you be blessed by the Lord; for you have had compassion on me.
>
> [23:21]

Saul, in spite of everything, still the courageous defender of Israel against the Philistines (23:27 f.).

The death of Samuel (25:1).

The charming story, intimately reflecting the times, of David, Nabal and Abigail (ch. 25), concluded, appropriately, with the succinct notice of David's loss (?) of Michal (25:44).

The stunning account of David's refusal to take matters of the kingdom and the covenant—Yahweh's kingdom, Yahweh's covenant—into his own hands in his refusal to take the life of Saul, Yahweh's anointed (ch. 26, compare the duplicate account, ch. 24); David's magnificent speech, fraught with implications for the story of Israel's faith (26:17-20, cf. 24:8-15); and Saul's response eloquently portraying not only the deep sickness that possessed him, but the stark tragedy of Israel's first king who would—*but could not*—realize his intrinsic greatness (26:21-25, cf. 24:16-22).

David's flight (again?—see 21:12 ff.) to Achish of Gath, his occupation of Ziklag, his activities there and his relationship with Achish (ch. 27).

The tragic Saul again, unable to elicit any response from Yahweh (28:6) and knowing therefore (always in the faith of Israel) the most extreme aloneness and alienation, a living death; Saul turning to the dead (28:7 ff.) in the person of a medium of Endor, in an action which he himself had at some earlier time prohibited (28:3b); Saul hearing (as he and Israel apparently believed) the sentence of death from the dead Samuel (28:15 ff.) as earlier he had heard the sentence of expulsion from the living Samuel.

David's release (it must have been to him a reprieve) from the Philistines en route to the battle against Israel in which Saul and Jonathan lose their lives (ch. 29); the sack of Ziklag by Amalekites in his absence (30: 1 ff., and note especially vv. 6-8); the successful pursuit (the Amalekites do not significantly appear again on the

pages of Old Testament history) ; and the highly judicious decision arrived at (30:21 ff.).

Saul's death—hardly suicide; Israel's total defeat; and the brave
act of gratitude by the men of Jabesh-gilead (ch. 31).

The stray Amalekite (!) reporting (falsely?) the death of Saul
and Jonathan to David (II Sam. 1:6-10); David's violent response
(1:15); David's deep sorrow and sense of breavement not only in
the loss of Jonathan, but of Saul (1:11 f., 17); and David's lament,
unsurpassed in world literature, acknowledged on every hand to
be the original composition of David himself (1:19 ff.).

David's establishment at Hebron as king over Judah, the southern confederation of tribes, probably with the consent of the
Philistines, even their approval (2:1-4); David's generous and
unimpeachably sincere (albeit politically astute) message of appreciation to Jabesh-gilead vv. 4b-7).

The re-establishment of the house of Saul (2:8 ff.) in the territory of Gilead to the east of the Jordan by Saul's commander,
Abner, in the person of the weak Ishbosheth (better, Ishbaal or
Eshbaal, the *bosheth,* meaning "shame," being a later editorial
substitution in names compounded with *baal,* the most common
Canaanite term for deity); the tentative "game" of war (2:14)
between the troops of Abner and those of Joab, David's commander, and the vivid description of the circumstances of Asahel's
death at Abner's hands; and finally the concluding notice:

> There was a long war between the house of Saul and the
> house of David; and David grew stronger and stronger, while
> the house of Saul grew weaker and weaker.

[3:1]

David's insistence (difficult to understand in view of the
portrayal of Michal's character) that Michal be returned to him
(3:13 ff.): is it possible that David wants Michal, the daughter
of Saul, as a reinforcement to his kingship?

The confirmation of Abner's expressed apprehension at having
to kill Asahel (2:22): deserting to David, he himself dies under

the binding custom of blood revenge at the hands of Asahel's brothers (3:30).

David's sincere (but again, astute) lament over Abner, reflecting not only David's continuing loyalty to the house of Saul, but his concern to unite the kingdom by winning over the adherents of Saul (3:31-39).

The same act of loyalty to Saul and Jonathan in the violent recompense of men who take the life of Eshbaal (Ishbosheth, 4:12).

The request that David rule over the northern tribes of Israel (5:1 ff.); the remarkable feat of the capture of the city of Jerusalem, in Canaanite (Jebusite) hands until now, and the stratagem by which this was accomplished (vv. 6-10).[6]

David, the historian, and Israel's understanding of the meaning of these events culminating in David's rule over the united kingdom:

> David perceived that Yahweh had established him king over Israel, and that he had exalted his kingdom for the sake of his people Israel.
>
> [5:12]

The Philistines' discovery, apparently for the first time, that David is no vassal! (5:17-22).

The revealing story, in intimate touch with the religious mind and practice of the times, of the bringing of the ark of the covenant into the capital city of Jerusalem (6:1-16); Michal's bitter scorn of David (vv. 16, 20); and the implication of divine judgment upon her (v. 23).

II Sam. 7 represents a later source than the bulk of what we have just outlined; but if we are concerned with Old Testament history, we are also concerned with the faith of Israel reflected in her historical writings, regardless of when the particular historical narrative assumed its present form. This chapter frankly represents the prophet Nathan as being in the wrong when he renders a decision *on his own* (vv. 1-3). His own word to the king is premature, and in error. The "Word of Yahweh" countermands Nathan's word (vv. 4 ff.). The account reflects the view that the truth spoken by a prophet, if it is the truth, does not come from the prophet himself, as a result of his own insight and genius, but from Yahweh, and by His Word.

We ought also to note that while the words of David's prayer (vv. 18 ff.) are hardly his in a literal sense, the general quality of the prayer is an accurate testimony to the inestimable significance of David for the life, vitality and spread of Yahwism.[7] Indeed, if any credence at all is to be given to the parallel account of the history of David in Chronicles—and we think it is—David had considerably more to do with the ultimate erection of the Temple than the Kings account would indicate (see I Chron. 28:11-19).

The notice of II Sam. 8:15 stands as an appropriate conclusion to the first phase of David's life and history:

So David reigned over all Israel; and David administered justice and equity to all his people.

C. DAVID (II SAM. 9-20; I KINGS 1-2)

II Sam. 9-20 has been described as "the unsurpassed prose masterpiece of the Hebrew Bible."[8] Together with I Kings 1-2, certainly by the same author, it is written, if not by an eyewitness, by one who stands very close and in intimate relationship to the events described.

Chapter 9 recounts David's kindness to the last surviving member of the house of Saul, the lame son of Jonathan (see II Sam. 4:4), here named Mephibosheth, but more accurately called Meribbaal (as in I Chron. 8:34 and 9:40). David's goodness here must be weighed against the tragic execution

—to be sure, "justified" in the ancient scheme of blood revenge—of other surviving members of the line of Saul in II Sam. 21, an episode almost certainly occurring in the earlier years of David's reign. Chapter 10 gives a vivid picture of Joab's (and David's—see 10:15 ff.) remarkable generalship in battle. It shows us too a surprising dimension in the character of David's loyal and competent commander-in-chief, Joab, who says, when the battle is set against him,

Be of good courage, and let us play the man for our people, and for the cities of our God; and *may Yahweh do what seems good to him.*

[10:12]

1. *Late one Afternoon . . . (II Sam. 11-12)*

In the spring of the year, the time when *kings* go forth to battle, *David* sent *Joab.* . . . It happened, late one afternoon, when David arose from his *couch.* . . .

[11:1-2]

Our historian not only knows the ways of David; he also knows the ways of language, and how to use it economically. As a comparable example of the writer's sensitive portrayal of the David-Joab relationship we cite now his notice that when the Ammonite city of Rabbah is ready for the ax the ever-loyal Joab sends for the king to strike the final blow and take the credit (12:26 ff.)!

Any attempt to adorn this story would be the rankest literary sacrilege. No word, no phrase, no subtle implication relieves the character of the king as adulterer and murderer. Correspondingly, there is not a whisper to diminish the man Uriah. He is a Hittite; but so far from employing this notice in derogation, the narrator assumes that his readers will understand the significance of Uriah's name: in token of "naturalization," he has taken a *Yah*weh-name, Uri-*yah* ("Yahweh is my light," or, perhaps, simply "Yahweh is light"). His loyalty to David, to Joab and to Israel, his integrity, and his great stature as a man are forcefully portrayed here; the inclusion of his name in one of the lists of David's most renowned warriors attests to his achievement in Israel's military establishment (see II Sam. 23:39).

Nathan, who replaces Samuel as prophetic spokesman in the story, is precisely and courageously in the line of Israel's unique prophetic succession. The prophetic act is divinely motivated, if not impelled (12:1). The prophet speaks not his own but the given word—"thus says the Lord . . ." (12:7). The prophetic condemnation is based not alone on the violation of a man-to-man relationship, but, since all life is judged by the righteousness of God, upon the violation of the divine-human relationship—"Why have you despised the word of the Lord, to do what is evil in *his* sight?" (12:9). And the judgment of God is unequivocally declared (12:10 ff.).

The judgment on David is strikingly appropriate. Again in the literature of Israel the "punishment fits the crime."

You have smitten Uriah the Hittite with the sword, and have taken his wife to be your wife [12:9]. . . . Now therefore the sword shall never depart from your house [v. 10]. . . . I will raise up evil against you *out of your own house* [v. 11].

We recall something of the same appropriateness of judgment upon Saul. His sin was disobedience; his judgment, expulsion from the kingship and separation from Yahweh. David's sin of violence is judged with violence (the sword does not depart from his house); and for his sin in the intimacy of sex, David is plagued with evil out of his own house, by tragedy within his own family.

If the story of Saul recalls to mind man's sin of disobedience in the Garden, his expulsion from it, and his separation from Yahweh (Gen. 3), the story of David bears an imprecise but suggestive resemblance to the Cain-Abel narrative of Gen. 4. There is no valid external reason for the sin of either Cain (see Gen. 4:6, 7a) or David. Neither acts under provocation—or rather, both commit the act of violence under provocation from within themselves. To David as well as to Cain, Yahweh might have said, "Sin is couching at the door; its desire is for you, but you must master it" (Gen. 4:7b). Neither Cain nor David does master it, and the sins of both lead to violence. Both commit a violent act within the existing community, which both understand as derived from Yahweh, as owing its very existence to him. David's sin is also against his brother, his covenant brother "Uri-yah." If Cain is his brother's keeper, certainly King David, of all people in the community of Israel, is the keeper of Bathsheba and Uriah. Both Cain and David admit their guilt—Cain, to be sure, by implication (Gen. 4:13). The judgments against the two are essentially the same. David soon suffers evil out of his own house. He becomes a fugitive, driven out (in a very real sense from the face of Yahweh; so, II Sam. 15:24-26) by his own son, Absalom. And, in both cases, the same limitation is set upon the judgment: both Cain and David are assured that their *lives* will be divinely protected (Gen. 4:15, II Sam. 12:13).

This general similarity between the two stories does not necessarily mean that one story was derived from the other, although it seems likely that both written accounts originated in the tenth century. Nor does it mean that the facts in the David story have been distorted in order to make it conform with the Cain-Abel myth. The similarity does, however, point up the coherence and the unity of the faith of Israel, a faith that preserves myths and records history with a consistent perspective and understanding. As in faith Israel sees the broken human community (both God-man, Gen. 3, and man-man, Gen. 4) in the Genesis myths, so in faith Israel surely sees the brokenness of her own community in Saul (God-man) and David (man-man). Of course, in Israel the king is never *merely* an individual. He *is* Israel. In his sin Israel sins; in his judgment Israel is judged. At the same time, the king is *also* himself, an individual man, a covenant person. Israel does not see this as an either/or proposition. The king is both one *and* many, bearing in himself the totality of the nation just as the three principle characters in Gen. 3-4 are at once themselves and all men.

Recall these lines of T. S. Eliot:

> What life have you if you have not life together?
> There is no life that is not in community,
> And no community not lived in praise of GOD.[9]

It happened late one afternoon. It has happened in human history on repeated afternoons. David or Cain or any one of countless others said to a brother, "Let us go out into the field." And when they were in the field, he rose up against his brother and killed him. Then God said, "The voice of your brother's blood is crying to me. . . ."

David and Cain. Israel and mankind. In the faith of Israel, Yahweh is Judge in history.

2. Absalom had a Beautiful Sister . . . (II Sam. 13-14)

Nathan said to David, ". . . Thus says the Lord, 'Behold, I will raise up evil against you out of your own house. . . .' "

[II Sam. 12:7, 11]

As Saul's historian sees the king's sin of disobedience as the turning point of his reign (I Sam. 13 and 15), so David's historian understands that the life and career of the king turn upon his sin with Bathsheba. Up to this point, David's life has been, on the whole, singularly blessed, emphatically triumphant. But from this point on the days of his years are lived under unremitting harassment. Formerly, David's life had been "bound in the bundle of the living" (I Sam. 25:29); now it is bound in the bundle of the suffering.

In Nathan's incisive parable (II Sam. 12:1-5), David has been brought to see clearly his own shameful part in the conventional triangle of David-Bathsheba-Uriah. He must now witness a grotesquely modified re-enactment of the situation, in which his role of adulterer is played by his son Amnon, his role of murderer by his son Absalom, and the role of the violated woman by his daughter Tamar. The murdered member of the triangle is, again, his son Amnon. The life of David is in truth now bound in the bundle of the suffering, the anguished, the tormented!

The historian rightly leaves the reader to his own devices in assessing Absalom's motives for murdering his brother; but we wonder if it is only the indignation of the full brother over his sister's shame that leads him to violence. Looking ahead to Absalom's arrogant rebellion against his father, so soon to follow, we wonder if this is not also, and perhaps chiefly, a convenient excuse for removing the king's oldest son Amnon, who might have proved an obstacle to Absalom's own consuming ambition. Then, too, although marriage with a half-sister is expressly forbidden in later legislation (see Lev. 18:9), it is clear that in David's time Amnon might have married Tamar, had he wished. And apparently it would have been with Tamar's consent, since she herself suggests it in remarkably gentle words (II Sam. 13:12 f.).

We note, too, that the Septuagint (the Greek translation

of the Hebrew Bible) includes a line at the end of II Sam.
13:21 that may well be authentic. The Hebrew text reads:

> When King David heard all these things [i.e., what had hap-
> pened between Amnon and Tamar], he was very angry.
>
> [II Sam. 13:21]

The Septuagint adds:

> Yet he did not vex the spirit of Amnon his son, for he loved
> him because he was his first-born.

The author might have added—King David remembered
the shame of his own guilt. If the Septuagint is authentic,
it suggests how remarkably indulgent David was toward
Amnon, and, apparently, toward all his children.

Following his murder of his brother Amnon, Absalom
goes into exile for three years. He is given refuge by his
mother's father, the king of Geshur (probably a district of
Bashan east of the Jordan). What of the king during these
years? The historian compresses three years of David's life
into a single verse:

> And the spirit of the king longed to go forth to Absalom; for
> he was comforted about Amnon.
>
> [II Sam. 13:39]

David's historian never insults the perceptiveness of his
readers. His only commentary lies in his incomparably deft
and skillful use of language. He is a member of the community of Israel. He writes about that community. He writes
for that community. He and the Yahwist employ essentially
the same techniques in imparting form, coherence and interpretation to their literary works. Both remain faithful to
what is "given"—the Yahwist to the traditions which he em-
ploys, and the historian to the events which he records. Both

narrators bring to bear a literary and interpretative artistry
by the primary means of a highly perceptive selectivity and
arrangement of material.

Chapter 14 concludes what the narrator obviously regards
as the most significant episode in a seven-year span of David's
mature reign (see 13:23, "after two full years"; 13:38, "Absalom [was in Geshur] three years"; 14:28, "Absalom dwelt
two full years in Jerusalem, without coming into the king's
presence"). These seven years have been compressed and
unified into a single event. It is announced in 13:1 with
the words,

> Now Absalom, David's son, had a beautiful sister. . . .

It is concluded with the last verse of chapter 14, with the
statement that Absalom

> came to the king, and bowed himself on his face to the ground
> before the king; and the king kissed Absalom.

We may remark in chapter 14 the reflection of Joab's deep
devotion to David (14:1); the implication of the king's accessibility to his subjects (v. 4); the stratagem which Joab
and the wise woman of Tekoa employ, strongly reminiscent
of Nathan's parable (vv. 5 ff.); the brilliantly vivid and authentic quality in the description of the interview; David's
intimate understanding of Joab (v. 18 f.); the name Absalom
gives to his daughter (! v. 27); the spoiled Absalom's wan-
tonly rude treatment of Joab and Joab's docile (now, but
not later!) acceptance of it (vv. 28 ff.).

3. Absalom got Himself a Chariot. . . . (II Sam. 15-20)

The complexities of government in Israel increased with
David's years; and now, obviously, he is unable to give his
subjects the personal attention that they had enjoyed during

the period of the early monarchy. Absalom capitalizes on this easiest of all popular criticisms of the king, and works quietly for four years at gaining popular support for himself (15:1-6).

It is difficult to believe that David was unaware of Absalom's rebellious intentions. In fact, the historian later records the anonymous, but certainly accurate, testimony that "there is nothing hidden from the king" (18:13). David always had the support of a large group of intimate and intensely loyal friends, even in the days, soon to come, of his greatest danger. It is even doubtful that David was fooled by Absalom's pretext for going to Hebron (15:7-9). One suspects that David simply refused to face the seditious implications of his son's actions.

Absalom's choice of Hebron as headquarters for launching his rebellion was shrewd indeed. Hebron was an ancient and venerated religious center, but, even more important, it had been David's capital for more than seven years. Even David, with all his political astuteness, would not have been able to move the seat of Israel's government to Jerusalem without leaving behind some disaffection in Hebron. Absalom must have doubted, too, that David could ever bring himself to attack Hebron.

Absalom was an arrogant man, consumed with ambition; but he was no fool. He set about winning over Ahithophel, a court counselor of David whom the narrator regards as the personification of wisdom:

Now in those days the counsel which Ahithophel gave was as if one consulted the oracle of God; so was all the counsel of Ahithophel esteemed, both by David and by Absalom.

[II Sam. 16:23]

Obviously David could have launched a successful attack on Hebron at once. Although "the people with Absalom kept increasing" (15:12), David's military organization under Joab was intact, and it was a trained and seasoned unit. But there are two obvious reasons why David could not bring himself to crush the rebellion: (1) his loving indulgence of his son—he could not himself force the attack; (2) his tenderness toward Hebron, its inhabitants and its sanctuary.

No other episode is more profoundly revealing of the man himself than David's evacuation of Jerusalem. This same episode also reveals the consummate personal loyalty of those who knew David best and who served him most intimately. The exchange between David and Ittai is all the more moving when we remember that Ittai is a foreigner, a Philistine, apparently in command of "the six hundred Gittites who had followed [David] from Gath" (II Sam. 15:18).

Then the king said to Ittai . . . , "Why do you also go with us? Go back, and stay with the king [Absalom!]; for you are a foreigner, and also an exile from your home. You came only yesterday [not, of course, to be taken literally], and shall I today make you wander about with us, seeing I go I know not where? Go back, and take your brethren with you; and may Yahweh show steadfast love and faithfulness to you."

But Ittai answered the king, "As Yahweh lives, and as my lord the king lives, wherever my lord the king shall be, whether for death or for life, there also will your servant be."

[II Sam. 15:19-21]

Again, the narrative itself, as read by the sympathetic and sensitive reader, constitutes its own best commentary; and again, therefore, we call brief attention to points in the biblical text which, in our judgment, ought to be specially noted:

The maturity and depth of David's faith. He will not hold the ark as a personal talisman. He sends it back, with these words:

If I find favor in the eyes of Yahweh, he will bring me back . . . . but if he says, "I have no pleasure in you," behold, here I am, let him do to me what seems good to him.

[15:25 f.]

The priests Abiathar and Zadok, loyal to David, return to Jerusalem with the ark (15:27 f.) to be joined soon by Hushai, "David's friend" (a court title for an official adviser—15:32 ff.). If David's spirit is broken (note 15:30) he is still able to exercise the astute powers of strategy always characteristic of him.

Which is the liar, Ziba, the servant of Meribbaal (Mephibosheth, 16:1-4), or Meribbaal (see now 19:24-30)?

David and Shimei, Scene I: the stature of David, the man, portrayed under the despicable Shimei's abuse (16:5-14). The depth of David's faith is again evident (16:12); and the gentleness of David is all the more remarkable when we remember that these are his most miserable hours. In some respects, these are also his most valiant hours.

What ought we to make of Absalom's remark upon meeting Hushai (16:16 f.)? Is it possible that the statement carries the inference of concern on the part of the son for his father? Does this suggest some relief (perhaps with 14:27) in the callousness of the character of Absalom?

Absalom's irrevocable commitment to the act of rebellion. Upon Ahithophel's shrewd advice, he "goes in" to his father's concubines. This is the final gesture of rebellion. Absalom has taken the place of his father—"in the sight of all Israel" (16:20-22).

The outcome of David's strategy. Absalom accepts the false counsel of Hushai against the strategically sound counsel of Ahithophel. And Ahithophel, knowing that the plan cannot succeed and that the rebellion is doomed, plays the role not of the spoiled child but of the unqualified realist. He takes his own life (17:1-23).

David at Mahanaim, in the east Jordan territory of Gilead. It is significant that David is given refuge, and cordial refuge, in the place where earlier Abner had set up the throne of Saul's house for

Eshbaal (Ishbosheth). The notice here (17:27-29) is an eloquent commentary on the thorough way in which David won by gentleness and kindness the allegiance of Saul's supporters.

David in anguish for the safety of Absalom (18:1-5). It is not a king, not the mighty David of old, who stands alone at the side of the gate pleading with Joab, Abishai and Ittai, "Deal gently for my sake with the young man Absalom." It is the pathetic figure of a father who loves even the son who would take his life.

The battle is joined (18:6 ff.). Absalom is fast caught in a tree, not by his hair, as artists (?) persistently portray it, but by his head (18:9). Joab is—Joab! His loyalty to David is absolutely unimpeachable. But he is tough and practical, and he sometimes, as here, makes his own decisions as to what is best for the king (18:10-15).

A difficult text in 18:18. The Septuagint reading differs from ours, giving support to the sense that *David* had the Absalom memorial erected. And the notice that Absalom had no sons is in conflict with II Sam. 14:27, which may be a late addition. But the present verse is not above suspicion and its text has suffered some abuse in transmission.

Ahimaaz and the Cushite (probably Egyptian) and the bearing of the report of Absalom's death to David (18:19-32). Here again is the vivid, intimate character portrayal, the subtle inferences, the effective dialogue which the narrator draws with such skill. Joab and (almost too late) Ahimaaz fear the old David who more than once struck down in wrath the bearer of tragic news. But that David is no more.

The description of the broken David:

> And the king was deeply moved, and went up to the chamber over the gate, and wept; and as he went, he said, "O my son Absalom, my son, my son Absalom! Would I had died instead of you, O Absalom, my son, my son!"
>
> [18:33]

Joab is—Joab. When victory is turned by the king's grief into mourning, it is Joab—surely no one else could have done so—

who shocks the king back into a state of responsibility and self-control, back into reality (19:1-7). And here the narrator betrays his genius in what he does *not* say. When the rebuke is administered, we read,

> Then the king arose and took his seat in the gate.
>
> [19:8a]

The self-abuse of those among the northern tribes who have participated in or countenanced the rebellion of Absalom (19:8 cf.). In effect they say, "What fools we have been! Let us escort the king back to the capital!"

The betrayal of David's partiality to the South, where no such spontaneous demonstration has yet appeared, in David's words to Zadok and Abiathar:

> Say to the elders of Judah, "Why should you be the last to bring the king back to his house, when the word of all Israel has come to the king?"
>
> [19:11]

David and Shimei, scene II (19:16-23): the stature of David the man portrayed no less than in the first scene (16:5-14). Here the stature of David the king is also portrayed, as it is in the two episodes which immediately follow (the settlement of the Ziba-Meribbaal controversy, vv. 24-29; and the good Barzillai's farewell of David, vv. 31-40.)

Sheba's short-lived rebellion. Obviously David has not succeeded in fully unifying North and South (19:41-43). His partiality to Judah angers some in Israel, and Sheba, a Benjaminite representing one of the northern tribes, enlists these malcontents in an act of secession (20:1 f.), although hardly on the scale suggested in the phrase "all the men of Israel" (v. 2). Now David demotes Joab and makes Amasa, Absalom's former general, commander-in-chief (so, almost certainly, the import of 20:4). And again, Joab is—Joab (20:4-10). If the notice of I Chron. 2:16 f. is correct, David had two sisters (perhaps only half-sisters but presumably daughters of Jesse): one, Zeruiah, was the mother of Joab,

Abishai and Asahel; the other, Abigail, was the mother of Amasa. This would mean not only a close relationship between David and Joab (and the same relationship between David and Amasa) but an even closer kinship between Joab and Amasa. It may be that the narrator acknowledged the close blood ties between Joab and Amasa in 20:9. But it is strange indeed that in such a patently well-informed history as we have in II Sam. 9-20 and I Kings 1-2, there is nothing that reflects the narrator's awareness of Joab and David's close blood relationship. II Sam. 17:25, the only other notice which gives us any clue as to the identity of Zeruiah, also sees her as the mother of Joab and the sister of Abigail (Amasa's mother—not to be confused with Nabal's widow and David's wife, I Sam. 25); but both women are daughters, not of Jesse (David's father) but of one Nahash, presumably David's friend the king of Ammon (see our comment above on II Sam. 10). Should we substitute the name "Jesse" for "Nahash" in II Sam. 17:25, or is I Chron. 2:16 f. in error? Whatever the answer to the question of David's relationship to Joab and Amasa, Joab's cold-blooded murder of Amasa is the brutal and repugnant violence of one grandson against another—whether the grandfather be Nahash or Jesse! It is certainly not our intention to "improve" the character of Joab. His adroit, if nasty, dispatch of Amasa does not even have the justification of blood revenge which obtained in his murder of Abner, who, we recall, had under some real compulsion taken the life of Joab's brother Asahel (II Sam. 2:18 ff.). Yet the murder of Amasa "fits" the consistent Joabian role! If Joab is personally ambitious, he is also convinced that he himself is David's best and most loyal commander. The decisive factor in crushing Sheba is speed—and Amasa has proved his incompetence (20:5). To the eminently practical Joab, there is only one solution. He effects it at once!

This is the most appropriate place for us to make another comment on the relationship of David to the sons of Zeruiah, a relationship involving tension. At least three times in the narratives about David, he speaks out in anger, annoyance and even frustration at their violent ways. Upon the death of Abner, Saul's commander, David composes a dirge which ends with the line

as one falls before the wicked [Joab!] you have fallen.

[II Sam. 3:34b]

And the deeply disturbed king then says to his servants:

Do you not know that a prince and a great man has fallen this day in Israel? And I am this day weak, though anointed king; these men the sons of Zeruiah are too hard for me. Yahweh requite the evildoer according to his wickedness!

[II Sam. 3:38 f.]

And twice, in the scenes with Shimei (II Sam. 16:10 and 19:22), when Abishai counsels violence, David bitterly deplores the spirit that longs to resolve every problem by force in the words

What have I to do with you, you sons of Zeruiah!

David himself would build and unify the kingdom quietly and slowly by kindness, mercy, love and forgiveness. The sons of Zeruiah would build and unify the kingdom by purge and violence. One can hardly escape the implications of an antithetical relationship between David the king and the sons of Zeruiah. The Chronicler, rewriting the history centuries later, either fails to see, or ignores, the tension. The sons of Zeruiah are never once reprimanded in the Chronicler's history (see I Chron. 11, 18, 26 and 27).

4. Now King David was Old . . . (I Kings 1-2)

As happened in the case of a number of books in the Old Testament, material which the editors could not appropriately insert elsewhere, they placed at the end of the book. I and II Sam. were originally a single book and in the closing chapters (II Sam. 21-24) we have a miscellaneous collection of writings, some old and reliable (21:1-14, 21:15-22 and 23:8-39, and ch. 24), some (22:1-23:7) relatively late.

The remarkable historical narrative of II Sam. 9-20 is

continued and concluded in I Kings 1-2, with an account of David's last days, Adonijah's abortive attempt to take the throne, and Solomon's accession.

To class Adonijah as a pretender and to compare him with Absalom, as some interpreters would do, is hardly warranted. He is next in line for the throne (I Kings 1:6 and 2:22); and it is a fair inference from the narratives that until David's senile period, Adonijah was his father's choice. If he had strong and influential opposition (including Nathan the prophet, 1:8), we also note that two of his supporters are Joab and Abiathar, both intensely loyal to David. Abiathar was the sole survivor of the priestly family of Eli and, like Joab, played a very important role in David's career. It is hard to believe that either man would have supported any aspirant to the throne not approved by David.

Since David is obviously in his dotage, one strongly suspects that the chief conspirators, Nathan and Bathsheba (Solomon's mother), are putting words into David's mouth which he never spoke:

Nathan said to Bathsheba . . . "Go in at once to King David, and say to him, 'Did you not, my lord the king, swear to your maidservant, saying, "Solomon your son shall reign after me, and he shall sit upon my throne"? Why then is Adonijah king?' Then while you are still speaking with the king, I also will come in after you and confirm your words."

[I Kings 1:11-14]

And it is certainly significant that the narrator never suggests that Nathan's actions in this case are in response to the prophetic word of Yahweh. This is again (as in II Sam. 7:1 ff.) a Nathan acting on his own. If an illegitimate claim is made and substantiated it is not that of Adonijah, but Solomon.

I Kings 1 is a busy and trying day for an old man tottering on the edge of the grave.

> So Bathsheba went to the king into his chamber [v. 15]. While she was still speaking with the king, Nathan the prophet came in [v. 22]. Then King David answered "Call Bathsheba to me." So she came [28]. King David said, "Call to me Zadok the priest, Nathan the prophet, and Benaiah. . . ." So they came before the king [v. 32].

It is no wonder that David dies in the next chapter!

The plot is successful. The conspirators elicit the authoritative word from the lips of the senile king, and Solomon reigns in David's stead. I Kings 2 must also be read in the light of the narrator's deft art and impartial description and in awareness that vv. 3-4, 10-12 and 27 are editorial (Deuteronomic) additions—as they obviously are. If David's charge to Solomon with respect to Joab and Shimei (vv. 4-9) actually represents a communication from David, one strongly suspects it to be an act of senility again contrived by Nathan and Bathsheba; for it is totally out of character with the king as we have known him. We understand very well, however, that Nathan and Bathsheba *and Solomon* would go to any lengths to secure David's authority for the purge; nor do we doubt that, if they failed to secure it, they alleged that it was given.

Solomon's first official acts are the expulsion of Abiathar and the brutal, unwarranted execution of Joab and Shimei. Those are the first of a number of conspicuous reversals of the policies of David and they symbolize in a deeply sinister way the tyrannical reign of Solomon.[10]

This section, II Sam. 9-20, I Kings 1-2, is the masterpiece of Old Testament history. It is intimately informed of the events and circumstances and persons which it treats; it is given phenomenally impartial expression; and it is wrought in literary form with unparalleled skill. But contrary to some,[11] we do not hold that this is a superlative prose masterpiece because of its "objectivity." Consonant with all biblical history, this is an interpretation of history, history interpreted in the strong perspectives of the covenant community.

In succeeding centuries this community increasingly remembers David not as a king but as the king, the Person in whom the fulfillment of the covenant hope is promised again, peculiarly symbolized, meaningfully previewed. The memory of David irresistibly shapes the images in which the faith of the community is projected. The day of covenant fulfillment will center in another "anointed one" (Messiah) of the *type* of David, the seed of David, the throne of David, the son of David.

Such is the image of hope in succeeding generations. But something of the hope is already conveyed in this early historian's work! Something of the hope is already implicit in his interpretation. David is a man who at his best is a Yahweh man, Yahweh's anointed. Here is one who at his best is an instrument of Yahweh's self-disclosure, possessed of Yahweh, revealing Yahweh; one on whom, peculiarly, the spirit of Yahweh rests,

> the spirit of wisdom and understanding,
> the spirit of counsel and might,
> the spirit of knowledge and the fear of Yahweh.
>
> [Isa. 11:2]

A thousand years later a "new" covenant community read this story of David and interpreted and understood its own central covenant Person as "son of David."

5. David and the "Son of David"

Repeatedly the writers of the New Testament endorse and reaffirm the relationship. Jesus is David's son—so in the

Gospels, Acts and Romans; and so in II Timothy, Hebrews and Revelation.

Their use of this term of relationship reflects their interpretation of Old Testament history and prophecy: David is regally, royally, the prototype of Christ. They also believe it literally, genetically: Jesus is of the seed of David. It may well be also that they meant it in a sympathetic sense: Jesus is David's son emotionally, spiritually, experiencially—in the positive meaning of the semitic idiom, like father, like son. If David is the royal prototype, if he is the physical ancestor, he is also the personal prototype of Jesus.

It is written:

Now [David] was ruddy, and had beautiful eyes, and was handsome. And Yahweh said [to Samuel], "Arise, anoint him; for this is he." Then Samuel took the horn of oil, and anointed him in the midst of his brothers; and the spirit of Yahweh came mightily upon David from that day forward.

[I Sam. 16:12 f.]

It is written of Jesus, the Son of David, that he

increased . . . in favor with God and man

[Luke 2:52]

and that he

came from Nazareth of Galilee and was baptized by John in the Jordan. And when he came up out of the water, immediately he saw the heavens opened and the Spirit descending upon him like a dove; and a voice came from heaven, "Thou art my beloved Son; with thee I am well pleased."

[Mark 1:9 ff.]

Like father, like son. Both refused the temptation to use their divinely given authority to alter the nature and design of the kingdom which both acknowledged to be God's kingdom. In the case of David, the theme is twice repeated. With

Saul at his mercy, he refuses the immediate satisfaction of his own ambition and declines to take the matters of the kingdom out of the hands of God and into his own hands. The temptation of Jesus, son of David, is appropriately on an infinitely grander scale, but the appeal of the temptation is the same; and its conclusion might without sacrilege be added at the close of the stories of David's temptation to take the life of Saul:

> And behold, angels came and ministered to him.
>
> [Matt. 4:11]

Like father, like son. Both take the city of Jerusalem in a full measure of triumph perhaps never known by any other conquerors. We have no record of David's actual entry into the city; but that it was truly a singular triumph is attested in all that subsequently transpired there. Jesus, the Son of David, moves into the city a thousand years later with ultimate consequences far more revolutionary. As the populace spread their garments in the way, Matthew appropriately records that they cried,

> Hosanna to the Son of David! Blessed be he who comes in the name of the Lord!
>
> [Matt. 21:9]

Like father, like son. At both extremes of this millennium, the shouting dies, the praises cease. Sweetness is turned bitter; devotion is become rebellion. David easily can, but will not, quench the little flame; for it is his son Absalom who revolts. He chooses, rather, voluntarily to quit the throne and the capital. It is written:

> David went up the ascent of the Mount of Olives, weeping as he went. . . .
>
> [II Sam. 15:30]

Jesus, the Son of David, has only quietly to turn about, shake off from his feet the dust of the streets of Jerusalem and return to his own Galilee. Instead, we read that when the disciples and Jesus had sung their last hymn together, they went out to the mount of Olives to a place which was called Gethsemane (Mark 14:26, 32).

Like father, like son. David commits the uncertain future to divine will. Refusing to take the ark with him, he says simply,

> If I find favor in the eyes of the Lord, he will bring me back . . . ; but if he says, "I have no pleasure in you," behold, here I am, let him do to me what seems good to him.
>
> [II Sam. 15:25 f.]

Jesus, the Son of David, dreading the immediate future like any other son of man, prays,

> . . . nevertheless, not as I will, but as thou wilt.
>
> [Matt. 26:39]

Like father, like son. David goes forth to his Gethsemane and to emotional crucifixion driven by a rebellious son.

> O my son Absalom, my son, my son Absalom! Would I had died instead of you, O Absalom, my son, my son!
>
> [II Sam. 18:33]

Jesus, the Son of David, suffers Gethsemane and crucifixion by other men equally in rebellion against their father. There was even a trial for both David and Jesus, the Son of David. As David evacuated the city of Jerusalem, a man of the house of Saul, named Shimei, cursed and threw stones at David as he and his men went along the way from the city. David forbade that any should touch him and later forgave him. Jesus, the Son of David, after formal trial, is brought before the whole battalion of soldiers, who, kneeling before him, mocked him, saying, "Hail, King of the Jews!" They spat upon him. They stripped him twice in the mocking exchange of garments and then, at last, led him forth (Matt. 27:27 ff.). His only response was given later: "Father, forgive them . . ." (Luke 23:34).

The community of the New Testament understood and accepted the interpretation of David as *the* king of ancient Israel, as peculiarly the Yahweh-man, as uniquely foreshadowing the fulfillment of the covenant purpose; and from that interpretation, already given in the history of David, they understood and interpreted the work and mission of Jesus.

Biblical history is often very good history, accurate history, sensitive history. It is also always interpreted history, whose direction and meaning is drawn directly from Israel's faith in the reality of the Yahweh covenant.

D. SOLOMON (I KINGS 3-11)

The actual dissolution of the united monarchy followed immediately upon the death of Solomon, but the process of the North's disaffection clearly began before David's death and continued throughout Solomon's reign with a steadily increasing intensity. The ultimate blame for the total alienation of Northern Israel falls directly upon Solomon.

At the conclusion of the Kings account of Solomon's reign, one of Israel's historians records the conviction that the tragedy of division was the direct judgment of God upon the apostasy of Solomon.

And the Lord was angry with Solomon, because his heart had turned away from the Lord. . . . Therefore the Lord said to Solomon, "Since this has been your mind . . . I will surely tear the kingdom from you. . . .

[I Kings 11:9, 11]

This judgment is immediately mitigated "for the sake of David" in two respects: (1) it will not be accomplished until after Solomon's death and (2) one tribe will be left to Solomon's son.

In view of this sweeping theological deprecation of Solomon, it may appear remarkable that the history retains the fabulous estimate accorded the king by tradition. In I Kings 3 we read a highly idealized and pious account of Solomon's humility and wisdom. Following the story of his thoroughly brutal purge in chapter 2, his prayer in 3:7-9 is, to say the least, out of character. Even more out of character are the words of Yahweh in vv. 12-14. In view of our own realistic appraisal of Solomon we are bound to read v. 15a with an emphasis hardly intended originally. "And Solomon awoke, and behold, it was a dream!" Appropriately to this build-up of Solomon, there follows at once that popular tale of the two harlots, intended to illustrate not only the great wisdom of the king, but also his accessibility to the meanest of the population. This about a king whose pride and ostentation are unparalleled in biblical history!

Chapter 4 makes the modest claim that Solomon "was wiser than all other men" (v. 31). It asserts in v. 20 that under Solomon "Judah and Israel were as many as the sand by the sea: they ate and drank and were happy." Elsewhere, however, it describes the elaboration of the structure of Israelite government (cf. 4:1 ff. with the relatively simple structure of officialdom under David in II Sam. 8:15 ff.), including the sinister notice that one Adoniram "was in charge of the forced labor" (v. 6). We also read of the division of the kingdom into twelve districts (shrewdly violating tribal divisions in a well-calculated effort to break down tribal loyalties) each with its overseer charged with the responsibility of providing sustenance for the royal establishment—a simple daily diet

(v. 22 f.) conservatively estimated as sufficient to feed between four and five thousand persons!

This same Solomon, allegedly wisest of the wise, "raised a levy of forced labor out of all Israel; . . . thirty thousand men" (5:13). Even if the draft was executed impartially, the bulk of the labor force was drawn from the North, with four or five times the population of Judah, and employed in the main in Solomon's ambitious building program in Jerusalem.

Chapter 6 describes the building of the temple. The temple area was no doubt considerable but the structure itself was small—sixty by twenty cubits, that is, probably, about ninety by thirty feet. It was used for individual, not congregational, worship and comprised two rooms; one—we might call it the main sanctuary—40 x 20 x 20 cubits (a double cube), and the other, the holy of holies, a perfect cube, 20 x 20 x 20 cubits,[12] containing the ark with its guard of two cherubim described very precisely in 6:23 ff. The temple was in reality not an Israelite but a Phoenician creation, achieved by virtue of Solomon's alliance with Hiram, king of Tyre and ruler of Phoenicia (ch. 5), and designed and executed by Phoenician architects and skilled craftsmen.[13]

There follows in chapter 7 the account of the building of Solomon's own royal palace, also Phoenician in design and execution, and a far more ambitious undertaking than the temple. Solomon's vast building program further included strategic fortifications at Jerusalem, Hazor, Meggido and Gezer (9:15 ff.); and the wealth, the splendor and the extensive commercial enterprise of Solomon are all reflected in the story of the Queen of Sheba's visit in chapter 10. There is no doubt that Solomon's was a dazzling reign and our composite record of that reign reflects his adulation by some in his own and subsequent generations.

But it was a magnificence bought at a terrific price and in

defiance of Yahwism. The present text of Kings, drawn from many sources, is the editorial achievement of Deuteronomic historians of the sixth century B.C. who, though regarding Solomon with nostalgic admiration, nevertheless incorporate material reflecting the perspective of stanch Yahweh loyalists. Of such is chapter 11, with the exception of certain Deuteronomic qualifications intended hopefully to mitigate the judgment of Solomon: so, e.g., v. 4, "when Solomon was old," and v. 6, "did not wholly follow Yahweh" (!).

Chapter 11 is comparable to the narratives of sin and judgment upon which the accounts of Saul and David turn (I Sam. 13 and 15, and I Kings 11). We are presented with three kings of the united monarchy—Saul, David and Solomon. Three sins are seen as ultimately determining the structures of the reigns—disobedience (Saul), violence (David), and now apostasy (Solomon). Three prophets proclaim the divine judgment—Samuel, Nathan and Ahijah. Saul's disobedience ends in his expulsion (cf. the story of Eden in Gen. 3); David's violence in tragic alienation within his own family (cf. the Cain-Abel narrative of Gen. 4); and Solomon's arrogant disregard of Yahweh in the disruption and confusion of the Israelite community (cf. the Babel account, Gen. 11).

It is Solomon who is judged in I Kings 11—but not Solomon alone, as it is also not Saul and David who alone are judged. In that ancient binding concept of community it is king and people who are judged. It is Solomon's but at once also all men's sins of apostasy, idolatry, the turning away of the human heart from God that brings the judgment of disruption, cleavage and tragic disunity.

And Yahweh said, . . . "Come, let us go down, and there confuse their language, that they may not understand one another's speech." So . . . they left off building the city [of God].

The essential language of Solomon and his prideful supporters in Judah became unintelligible to Northern Israel. The
covenant community was broken asunder and two centuries
later, the prophet Isaiah recalls the day of separation as an
event of singular tragedy (Isa. 7:17).

IV. PROPHECY

In the Days of Uzziah, Jotham, Ahaz and Hezekiah:
Isaiah 1-11, 17-22, 28-33

We have seen something of the covenant faith of Israel as it is expressed in Old Testament myth, legend and history. That faith finds its most dynamic articulation in the prophets.

In the strict sense of the word, there is no "typical" prophet. In the Hebrew canon of prophecy (the Latter Prophets) there are four "books" comprising fifteen names—Isaiah, Jeremiah, Ezekiel and the twelve "minor" prophets (the last twelve writings of our Old Testament, Hosea to Malachi). These fifteen writings vary in length, were written over a span of centuries from the eighth probably to the third B.C., are addressed to radically different historical situations, and certainly in their present form represent far more than fifteen writers. The creators of this literature do not always speak with one voice even on comparable points and the statement of one may sometimes stand in contradiction to that of another.

This is a study of Isaiah of Jerusalem whose prophetic ministry was performed in the latter half of the eighth century B.C. during the reigns of Uzziah, Jotham, Ahaz and Hezekiah, kings of Judah (Isa. 1:1). He, no more than any other prophet, is typical. Indeed, one suspects that the phrase "typical prophet" is a contradiction in terms. In the very nature of his being a prophet, a spokesman for Yahweh, he does not and cannot conform to a type. But Isaiah is *central* to Old Testament prophecy, perhaps as no other. How and why this is so will, we hope, become apparent.

The word of the prophet is characteristically addressed to the life and problems of the prophet's own community. It may involve (as it sometimes does) a process of extrapolation from the present scene, whereby divine commitment to the future is proclaimed in divine judgment or in redemption, or in both; or it may sweep backward in time to bring past events forcefully into the present with incisive relevance. But any reference to the past or the future is directly related to, or contingent upon, the present and it is intended primarily for the contemporary community.

The terms of the prophet's own existence and of his own immediate historical environment are of the essence. The prophet has no abstract word. What he passionately believes to be the revelation of Yahweh he *sees* in historical event and *understands* from the Word of Yahweh. There is no prophecy without history, and no understanding of the prophetic message apart from the history that calls it forth.

A. SURVEY OF JUDAH'S HISTORY THROUGH THE EIGHTH CENTURY B.C. (SEE I KINGS 12–II KINGS 20; ISA. 36-39)

The one Kingdom of Israel was severed immediately following the death of Solomon about 922 B.C.[1] With the bitter cry,

> To your tents, O Israel!
> Look now to your own house, David.
> [I Kings 12:16]

the northern tribes known collectively as Ephraim seceded from the union. Jeroboam became king in the North and Rehoboam, son of Solomon, ruled in Judah. Of the two resultant kingdoms, Judah was in territory and population much the smaller. Palestine's mountainous backbone running north and south between the Mediterranean and the Jordan valley is higher and more rugged in the south; and the city of Jerusalem, well fortified by nature against ancient methods of attack, stands at an elevation of about 2,700 feet. The routes of commerce between Egypt and the west crossed Israel (as the Northern Kingdom of Ephraim is called), not Judah. Judah was relatively isolated.

In part for these reasons, the Southern Kingdom was always culturally and religiously more homogeneous and conservative than Israel, and the continuity, with one brief interruption, of the Davidic rule provided a political stability never known in Israel.

But this is not to say that in the South every man sat peacefully under his own vine and his own fig tree contemplating in gratitude and thanksgiving the mercies of Yahweh. The riches of Judah were repeatedly plundered by Egypt, Edom and Assyria; life was threatened and harassed by Israel and Syria; the head that wore the crown in Judah often lay uneasy; and Yahwism had its apostasies and perversions.

Asa (c. 913-873), the second son of Rehoboam to occupy the throne, instituted a sweeping reform, the description of which in I Kings 15:9 ff. is convincing testimony of the influence upon Judah of the fertility cult of the Canaanite goddess Asherah. His son and successor, Jehoshaphat (c. 873-849), also remained a faithful Yahwist. During these two reigns, Judah gained a considerable degree of political stability, despite first her friction and later her costly alliance as junior partner with Israel.

The alliance was formed between Ahab and Jehoshaphat and was sealed with the marriage of Ahab and Jezebel's daughter Athaliah to Jehoshaphat's son Jehoram. Athaliah had a Yahweh name (Athali-yah = "Yahweh is strong"); but like her mother, she was an ardent protagonist of the cult of the Phoenician Baal, Melcarth. Following Jehoram's death, she exercised the influence of the queen mother upon her son Ahaziah until his violent death at the hands of Jehu in Israel (II Kings 9:21-28), when, shades of mother Jezebel, she proceeded to wipe out the royal family, including, of course, her own grandsons, and make herself queen. Thanks, however, to a counterscheme involving chiefly a sister of Ahaziah and her husband, Jehoiada, priest of Yahweh, one of Ahaziah's sons named Joash was hidden and, seven years later, successfully enthroned in a revolution that was at once political and religious. Jehoiada's role was decisive. Athaliah was slain and

> Jehoiada made a covenant between Yahweh and the king and people, that they should be Yahweh's people; and also between the king and the people. Then all the people . . . went to the house of Baal, and tore it down; his altars and his images they broke in pieces, and they slew Mattan the priest of Baal before the altars.
>
> [II Kings 11:17 f.]

The revolution of Jehu in Israel had its related counterpart in Judah, but Jehoiada's action on behalf of Yahwism in Judah was never condemned in later prophecy as Jehu's was, and with good reason. It was engineered with purposive restraint:

> All the people of the land rejoiced; and the city was quiet after Athaliah had been slain. . . .
>
> [II Kings 11:20]

Joash reigned, unfortunately without distinction, to the end of the century (c. 837-800). Like Jehu and Jehoahaz in Israel, he suffered bitterly from the ruthless aggression of

Hazael of Syria. His successor, Amaziah (*c.* 800-783), "killed ten thousand Edomites in the Valley of Salt" (II Kings 14:7) but, in an exchange of words heard in substance every day on elementary school playgrounds, provoked war with Israel that ended in Judah's disastrous defeat (14:8-14). Popular disaffection with the reigns both of Joash and Amaziah culminated in assassination. The Davidic line continued, now with some real distinction, under the grandson and son, respectively, Uzziah (or Azariah *c.* 783-742).

The Kings account of Uzziah's reign is one brief paragraph in length (Azariah, II Kings 15:1-7); but from Chronicles (II, ch. 26), from archaeological finds, and indirectly from the Southern prophets, Micah and Isaiah, we learn that Uzziah's reign was a period in Judah of vast expansion in territory, in commerce and in power, corresponding to the brilliance of the reign of Jeroboam II (*c.* 786-746) in the North. The Chronicler cites the restoration to Judah of Eloth (II Chron. 26:2) far to the south on the shore of the Red Sea. Eloth was near Ezion-geber, the site of a commercial enterprise of Solomon, whose facilities for refining copper in the area have been excavated. According to the Chronicler, Uzziah also conquered the Philistine territory on the Mediterranean coast (26:6), exacted tribute from Ammon (v. 8), built up the fortifications of Jerusalem (v. 9), and, among other accomplishments including activity in Arabia, developed the Negeb, the desert region to the south of Judah (v. 10). Archaeology provides some strong confirmation of the Chronicler's record. All indications point to the eighth century as one of unparalleled activity in the Negeb; and a seal of Jotham, Uzziah's son, has been recently excavated at Ezion-geber.[2]

There can be no doubt that the wealth and power of the crown in Judah under Uzziah was exceeded only by Solomon's reign at its peak. And the Chronicler, who sees only the glories of Solomon's rule, informs us that Uzziah's greatness was the reward of faithfulness to Yahweh (v. 5). Be that as it may, at least two Yahweh prophets, Isaiah and Micah, look out upon the life of Judah in the decades following Uzziah's reign with bitter reproach and with condemnations that must fall, in part, upon Uzziah. We are forced to conclude that, as in Solomon's day, Yahwists believed that the power, prestige, wealth and apparent security of the crown and the nation were bought at a price too dear —widening economic disparity between rich and poor, the ruthless exploitation of society's weaker members, a deepening acquisitiveness and an inevitably accompanying disregard of the justice and righteousness of Yahweh, the meaning of covenant, and the true practice of the Yahweh cult.

Before the end of his life Uzziah contracted leprosy, perhaps about 750 B.C. In all matters involving the public, his son Jotham acted in his place and, of course, succeeded to the throne when Uzziah died, about 742. II Kings 15 alludes to his accession only in passing (v. 7) and to his reign briefly (vv. 32 ff.). In terse fashion it describes the chaotic succession of kings in Israel following the death of Jeroboam II (c. 746) —Zechariah (six months), Shallum (one month), Menahem (ten years by the Kings count, but probably less; mentioned in an Assyrian inscription dated 738 B.C., confirming the notice of 15:19 that Menahem paid tribute to Assyria), Pekahiah (parts of two years), and finally Pekah, with a reign not of twenty years (so v. 27) but hardly more than two.[3] This violent program of royal succession was, in fact, a part of Israel's death throes.

In 745 B.C. the throne of Assyria fell to Tiglath-pileser III. Himself an able and aggressive ruler, he was followed in kind by Shalmaneser V (727-722) and Sargon II (722-705).

Sargon was succeeded by Sennacherib, considerably less able than his predecessors, who reigned in Assyria until 681. The second half of the eighth century, however, saw Assyrian power at its peak. The "Pul" of II Kings 15:19 is Tiglath-pileser, who exacted tribute in 738 not only from Menahem of Israel but from other small western states including Syria. There is no indication that Judah was among them.

About 735 B.C., Ahaz succeeded his father Jotham on the throne of Judah (II Kings 16:1). Pekah, king of Israel, and Rezin, king of Syria, both facing the immediate threat of the return of Assyrian armies, at once sought alliance with Ahaz and Judah, now the most stable, and probably the most powerful of the small western states. When Ahaz refused, they lay siege to Jerusalem in the obvious hope of deposing him and, with Judah under a ruler of their own choice, forming an allied army to meet Assyria. Ahaz found himself in a desperate situation. The notice of 16:3 that he sacrificed his own son probably refers to this time. But, folly of follies, he also sent to Tiglath-pileser requesting help. He did so against the advice of the prophet Isaiah (see Isa. 7), rightly given: Ahaz obligated himself unnecessarily, since Tiglath-pileser would certainly have dispatched his armies anyway. This independent action on the part of two vassal kings was obviously mutinous in intent.

So, in 734 B.C., Assyria was back in the west again with bitter vengeance. Damascus, the capital of Syria, and north Israel were plundered, and for the first time Assyria put in practice her policy of deportation of the potentially influential elements of conquered populations from whom leadership for revolt might subsequently be drawn. These were settled in other parts of the empire, their places taken by persons similarly uprooted elsewhere.

Judah was not invaded. But Ahaz was called to Damascus

in the role of a vassal and, in partial token of subservience, arranged to have a pagan altar constructed in Jerusalem (II Kings 16:10 ff.). The prophetic protest against political alliances was religiously motivated: it meant the compromise of Yahwism and the worship of alien deities.

By 732 B.C., Assyria had efficiently organized Syria and Israel, north of Samaria, into provinces and had replaced Pekah with Hoshea, who proved to be Israel's last king. Israel's end came quickly in 722 or 721 B.C.

In Judah, whose history is resumed in II Kings 18, Jotham is succeeded by Hezekiah about 725. This is a round number: the date remains uncertain. But one thing is very clear: from the time of Assyria's resurgence of power in the eighth century to the setting of her sun in the closing decades of the seventh, Hezekiah was the only king of Judah seriously to contest the domination of Assyria. He expressed his defiance in two ways. He instituted a vigorous religious reform, always in the ancient Near East a gesture of independence under such circumstances; and he undertook elaborate defense measures, including the strengthening of the outer fortifications of Jerusalem and the construction of the Siloam tunnel. II Kings 20:20 alludes to the tunnel briefly; a more detailed account is given in II Chron. 32. Jerusalem's chief source of water was the Gihon spring outside the city wall. The spring was made inaccessible to attackers and its waters were channeled in a subterranean tunnel cut through the soft limestone rock into the city. Workers, beginning at opposite ends, met in the middle; and someone, at the point of meeting, placed this inscription in the wall of the tunnel, now excavated:

The boring through is completed. And this is the story of the boring through: while yet they plied the drill, each toward his fellow, and while yet there were three cubits to be bored through, there was heard the voice of one calling to another, for there was a crevice in the rock on the right hand. And on the day of the boring through the stone-cutters struck, each to meet his fellow, drill upon drill; and the water flowed from the source to the pool for a thousand and two hundred cubits, and a hundred cubits was the height of the rock above the heads of the stone-cutters.

The tunnel is more than 1,700 feet in length. The workmen failed to meet precisely head-on, but it was for the time a superior feat of engineering.

In view of Hezekiah's show of defiance, it is remarkable that he escaped Assyrian chastisement and humiliation for so long a time. In 711 he was in all probability party to a rebellious coalition of states including, as we know from Assyrian records, Egypt and the Philistine city-state of Ashdod. Merodach-baladan, king of Babylon from 721-710, and again for six months in 705-704, may also have been involved. His embassy to Hezekiah described in II Kings 20:12 ff. must have been sent either in 711 or in 705: and it therefore preceded the devastating invasion of the west by Sennacherib in 701 (II Kings 18:13-19:36).

Assyrian wrath was poured mercilessly on the western states, including Egypt and Ethiopia, in 701. The co-operative effort at resistance was futile. Sennacherib, whose annals were recorded on clay cylinders now recovered by archaeologists, wrote in part of this campaign as follows:

As for Hezekiah, the Jew, who did not submit to my yoke, 46 of his strong, walled cities, as well as the small cities in their neighborhood, which were without number,—by escalade and by bringing up siege engines, by attacking and storming on foot, by mines, tunnels and breaches, I besieged and took. 200,150 people, great and small, male and female, horses, mules, asses, camels, cattle and sheep, without number, I brought away from them and counted as spoil. Himself, like a caged bird, I shut up in Jerusalem, his royal city. Earthworks I threw up against him,— the one coming out of his city gate I turned back to his misery. The cities of his which I had despoiled I cut off from his land and to Mitinti, king of Ashdod, Padi, king of Ekron, and Silli-bel, king of Gaza, I gave them. And thus I diminished his land. I added to the former tribute, and laid upon him as their yearly payment, a tax in the form of gifts for my majesty. As for Hezekiah, the terrifying splendor of my majesty overcame him, and the Urbi and his mercenary troops which he had brought in to strengthen Jerusalem, his royal city, deserted him. In addition to 30 talents of gold and 800 talents of silver, there were gems, antimony, jewels, large sandstones, couches of ivory, maple, boxwood, all kinds of valuable treasures, as well as his daughters, his harem, his male and female musicians, which he had them bring after me to Nineveh, my royal city. To pay tribute and to accept servitude he dispatched his messengers.

The Kings account of the siege agrees substantially, al-though not in all details, with that of Sennacherib, who, be it noted, does not claim the actual fall of Jerusalem. Three possible reasons for the lifting of the siege appear. The first is the payment of tribute. But according to II Kings 18:14-16, this was *before* the siege of Jerusalem and if in fact so, it hardly constitutes a reason for the lifting of the siege. After its payment, according to this biblical account, and before joining battle with the Egyptians at Eltekeh in southern Judah, Sennacherib expressed his continuing distrust of Heze-kiah in a note of sharp warning which Hezekiah interpreted as a threat to return and destroy the city of Jerusalem. If such were the true circumstances, it *is* remarkable that the Assyrian siege was abandoned short of the actual capitulation of Jerusalem. It would appear that the collapse of Judah's capital could have been accomplished then as easily as at any time in the period of Assyrian ascendancy. Morale in Jerusalem was at a near-record low. On every hand, surrounding city-states and nations were prostrate. In Judah itself, forty-six cities had been destroyed. No pride remained in Jerusalem: Hezekiah had stripped the temple, exhausted all wealth, and surrendered members of his own family in tribute.

Perhaps, as the Sennacherib inscription might imply, the besieging Assyrian forces were bought off with the tribute. The Kings account sees it differently.

A second possible reason for the abandonment of the siege is the notice of II Kings 19:7—the call of critical Assyrian military business elsewhere, a "rumor" of trouble in another part of the empire. A third possible reason is the sudden toll of death among the Assyrian forces by plague (the angel of the Lord, 19:35). The sequence and detail of events may now be irrecoverable and we do not doubt the influence of popular legend in the third possible explanation. But one fact is clear. Some who suffered through the siege—king Hezekiah and prophet Isaiah among them—believed that Assyria's departure, by whatever visible causes induced, was a Yahweh deed on behalf of his covenant people, in accordance with his own covenant purpose. The remarkable oracle (19:20-28) attributed to Isaiah (and if not from him certainly from a contemporary) states this faith with explosive force (cf. Isa. 10:5 ff.). Yahweh to Assyria:

> . . . I know your sitting down
>   and your going out and coming in,
>   and your raging against me.
> Because you have raged against me
>   and your arrogance has come into my ears,
> I will put my hook in your nose
>   and my bit in your mouth,

> and I will turn you back on the way
> by which you came.
>
> [19:27 f.]

Hezekiah survived to recoup some of his losses before his death about 686. He is one of only two kings of Judah (with Josiah, c. 640-609) to receive the unqualified endorsement of the Deuteronomic historians (II Kings 18:1-8). The evaluation is well made. If Isaiah found occasion, as certainly he did, to protest aspects of Judah's life during Hezekiah's long reign, prophet and king enjoyed for the most part a relationship of mutual respect, as witness Hezekiah's dependence upon Isaiah during the fearful days of Sennacherib's siege, and the story, augmented by legend, of Hezekiah's illness in II Kings 20.

Hezekiah's son and successor, Manasseh, was a man of totally different character. Biblical tradition records of him that he "shed very much innocent blood, till he had filled Jerusalem from one end to another" (II Kings 21:16). Extrabiblical tradition tells of the death of the aged Isaiah at Manasseh's instigation.

B. The Book of Isaiah

There are 66 chapters in Isaiah, as the book now stands in the Old Testament canon. As long ago as the 1780's scholars recognized that chapters 40-66 could not be the work of Isaiah of Jerusalem because they deal with, and reflect an intimate knowledge of, events in the sixth century B.C.

In chapters 1-39, chapters 36-39 are closely paralleled by II Kings 18-20, which we have just surveyed. While the prophet is prominently figured, these historical narratives are hardly from Isaiah and may well have been added to the book of Isaiah from Kings.

Chapters 34-35 are on a number of counts suspect. The perspective appears almost certainly to be later than Isaiah and it is possible and even probable that the two chapters were an original introduction to chapters 40 ff.

This leaves us with the first 33 chapters of the book. The precise analysis of this section is exceedingly complicated and fraught with controversy, but three general observations may be drawn. (a) The block of chapters, 1-33, does not constitute an original unit, but results from the compilation of several older collections of material, each of which was gathered at a different time and by different hands. Roughly, four such collections are represented:

> 1-12. In large part authentically Isaianic; and mainly from the prophet's earlier ministry.
>
> 13-23. Oracles for the most part against foreign nations with non-Isaianic material predominating.
>
> 24-27. An apocalyptic section, considerably later than Isaiah.
>
> 28-33. Isaianic material again predominating; and mainly from Isaiah's later years.

(b) The present order of oracle and incident within these collections is not chronological. It is sometimes impossible to date a given passage, and prophetic utterances separated in time, and even in reverse order, may sometimes be found side by side.[4]

(c) The teachings of Isaiah of Jerusalem were preserved, altered and augmented, and reapplied to the changing historical scene for at least the next several centuries by a continuing and self-perpetuating circle of disciples.[5] It is our judgment that in the present book of Isaiah much of the material admittedly not from Isaiah of Jerusalem is in a profound sense "Isaianic" in that it faithfully represents the essential theology of the eighth-century prophet.

C. THE MAN ISAIAH

What do we know, significantly, of the person of Isaiah?

(a) He was an urbanite. Isaiah knows best the life of the city —Jerusalem. Everything in his life that reflects his own personal experience supports this. Any intimate knowledge of his of the kingdom of Judah is confined to the city; his interest is always concentrated there. Indeed, his very language—the similes, metaphors and illustrations that he uses—betrays him as a man of urban mind and outlook.

(b) It is commonly assumed that Isaiah was a man of noble birth, related by blood to the wider royal family of Judah. We are reminded that he spoke unequivocally with men in high authority, from the king (e.g., Isa. 7) to the chief steward of the royal household (22:15 ff.). Isaiah's great freedom of movement is called in evidence, his air of assurance, his apparent escape from any serious form of persecution. Perhaps Isaiah was of Jerusalem's nobility; but if there is nothing to deny it there is, on the other hand, nothing to confirm it. We remember other prophets, before and after Isaiah, who spoke with courage and integrity in the face of the king. Other prophets were granted or fearlessly exercised freedom of movement. The forceful declaration, "Thus saith Yahweh," is of the essence of prophecy. And in the long history of Old Testament prophecy there is no recorded instance of the successful silencing of a major prophet. Some certainly suffered more public abuse than others or firmer opposition from the royal house; but Isaiah's counsel was on occasion categorically rejected by the king (so again Isa. 7), and he must have suffered more than once the cutting public derision to which he refers in 28:9 f. In the case of at least one prophet an apparent effort is made in an unusually extended genealogical introduction to establish royal lineage (Zeph.

1:1). Isaiah appears simply as "the son of Amoz." If he was of royal blood, canonical tradition evidently did not regard the matter as of any great consequence.

(c) He was married to a woman whom he refers to only once as "the prophetess" (8:3). He does not apparently mean a female prophet (although the term is later so used in the Old Testament of Huldah, II Kings 22:14), but simply the wife of a prophet (cf. Duke-Duchess). In Amos' day only a few decades earlier the term "prophet" was in disrepute in the Northern Kingdom and Amos disclaimed the title (Amos 7:14). Isaiah's use of the term in this way suggests perhaps that prophecy in Judah had fared better; or perhaps that the work and stature of an Amos had helped to restore the term to a place of respect.

(d) The prophet and prophetess, Isaiah and wife, had to our knowledge two sons, both named, as were Hosea's children, symbolically. The name of the first, Shear-jashub (7:3), means "a remnant shall turn" (that is, turn back again to Yahweh) or "a remnant shall return" (for the fulfillment of the covenant, and inferentially perhaps, from exile). It is a two-sided symbol, negative and positive. "Remnant" unmistakably implies divine judgment upon the nation and, at least as interpreted by Isaiah's disciples, catastrophic judgment falling upon the whole nation, Jerusalem included. We think Isaiah himself also envisioned it so. But on the other side, the symbol expresses the unquenchable biblical faith in divine redemption. Judgment is meted out, not vindictively nor as a merely punitive measure:

> I will turn my hand against you
>> and will smelt away your dross as with lye
>> and remove all your alloy.
>
>   [Isa. 1:25]

Judgment is a purifying fire necessitated by gross unfaithfulness in the covenant community, but positive in ultimate purpose. Yahweh is working redemptively in history: a remnant *will* return.

The second son is born and named when Ahaz and Judah are threatened by the Rezin-Pekah alliance, to which crisis the name (8:1-3) has immediate and positive reference. Mahershalalhashbaz is symbolically predictive of the overthrow of Judah's enemies: Damascus (Syria) and Samaria (Israel) will quickly become the spoil and prey of Assyria—"the spoil speeds, the prey hastes" is the meaning of the name. On the assumption that little Mahershalalhashbaz survived (quite an assumption, with such a name) we cannot but wonder whether Isaiah may not later have referred the name in a now negative symbolism to Judah herself. The name is not mentioned again—understandably. Our own private tradition has it that a number of the lad's playmates in Jerusalem became incurable stutterers.

This, then, we know about the man Isaiah—an urbanite prophet, at home in, and on intimate terms with, the life of Jerusalem, counselor (if not relative) of kings, married, the father of at least two children; and, certainly we ought to add, a man of passing eloquence. We doubt that Old Testament history ever produced a man more gifted in the use of language. Some of Isaiah's recorded oracles must be ranked with the most beautiful and majestic passages in the world's literature. But this is emphatically not the most significant measure of the stature of Isaiah.

D. The Prophet Isaiah

The vision of Isaiah the son of Amoz, which he saw concerning Judah and Jerusalem in the days of Uzziah, Jotham, Ahaz, and Hezekiah, kings of Judah. . . .

[Isa. 1:1]

The true measure of Isaiah's stature is his mind and faith. With phenomenal sensitivity and what we may describe only as inspired judgment, he extracts from Israel's total heritage her truest and most enduring insights, the unique qualities of her understanding of history, and the essence of her historical faith. We venture the claim not only that Isaiah is central to prophecy but that no prophet stands more nearly in the center of biblical theology nor anticipates in such comprehensive fashion many of the affirmations of the New Testament community. Isaiah's influence upon subsequent Old Testament theology and ultimately upon Christianity is incalculable.

In the year that King Uzziah died I saw the Lord sitting upon a throne, high and lifted up. . . .

[6:1]

So begins the account of Isaiah's call and commission to prophecy. So begins a description of the nearly indescribable —one man's sense of direct confrontation by Him whose glory fills the whole earth (v. 3). Chapter 6 has been appropriately called Isaiah's "most revealing page." In thirteen verses the prophet lays bare the totality of his faith. Every significant affirmation, elaborated elsewhere, is at least inferentially here.

This is not to say that Isaiah presents here—or in the sum of his oracles—a systematic theology. He does not think systematically; indeed, the Old Testament prophet never sees himself as *thinker* at all, but rather as *responder*. He is, in the bare, plain, nonphilosophical sense of the term, an existentialist. He responds pointedly and often passionately to the specific realities of his own existence—realities which in his understanding embrace without significant differentiation what we would call spiritual and physical phenomena. Isaiah's call is to him just as concrete an event as his meeting with Ahaz in the next chapter and for that very reason incomparably more intense: Ahaz is only a king; Yahweh is The King, Yahweh of hosts! (6:5). The one experience is as "historical" as the other. As he meets Ahaz when Rezin and Pekah "came up to Jerusalem to wage war against it" (7:1) so he sees the Lord "in the year that King Uzziah died." Both are events, dated and located. As he confronts Ahaz "at the end of the conduit of the upper pool on the highway to the Fuller's Field" (7:3) so he is confronted by Yahweh in "the temple" (6:1).

In the formal sense of the word, then, there can be no prophetic "theology." The prophet does not draw abstractions from the concrete, generalizations from the specific. His theology is practical, never theoretical. It is articulated in relation and response to particular events in his particular existence; and when the response is made, the prophet is usually so intensely and totally absorbed that he does not concern himself with the relationship between this and some other response. His theology, then, is not only not systematic: it may appear to us to be at points inconsistent.

Chapter 6 records perhaps the most significant moment, the most influential event, in Isaiah's life. If it is the first episode (c. 742 B.C.) in a long prophetic career, we suspect that the present account of it was created much later. We think it must represent Isaiah's recollection of his call from the vantage point of a prophetic career long in process, although there are many who would disagree with our judgment.

The only real problem in understanding and interpreting Isa. 6 is in vv. 9 ff., Yahweh's commission to the new prophet. It is clear that Isaiah did not know to what he would be

assigned when he answered with his emphatic "Here am I!
Send me" (v. 8). But in what follows it is equally clear, we
think, that he recalls, early or late in his ministry, a Yahweh
who speaks in bitter irony:

> Go, and say to this people:
> "Hear and hear, but do not understand;
> see and see, but do not perceive."
> Make the heart of this people fat,
>   and their ears heavy,
>   and shut their eyes;
> lest they see with their eyes,
>   and hear with their ears,
> and understand with their hearts,
>   and turn again and be healed.
>
> [v. 9 f.]

His is a prophetic ministry doomed from the outset to
futility and, worse, to the intensification of the very attitudes
which the prophetic mission would correct. If we could have
asked Isaiah, when he came thus to understand his prophetic
task, early or late, "Why go on with it at all?" we are sure
he would have given answer in the words of Amos (3:8), "The
Lord Yahweh has spoken; who can but prophesy?"

It is also clear from the call that Isaiah believed Judah's
historical judgment to be inescapable. The prophet asks
how long the perversity of Judah will continue, how long
this people will remain fat of heart, heavy of ear, and blind
of eye. Yahweh replies:

> Until cities lie waste
>   without inhabitant,
> and houses without men,
>   and the land is utterly desolate,
> and Yahweh removes men far away,

and the forsaken places are many
in the midst of the land.
And though a tenth remain in it,
it will be burned again. . . .

[6:11 ff.]

We seriously doubt that Isaiah regarded this threat as fulfilled by Sennacherib's invasion in 701 B.C. We are forced to conclude, from this and other references, that Isaiah, like Amos, was a prophet of doom.

We cannot systematize the theology of Isaiah; but we can easily see his strongest emphases, his dominant prophetic themes. We may list them as follows, recognizing that they are by no means mutually exclusive, that all are to some degree implicit in any one: The Covenant, the Holiness of Yahweh, the Pride and Perversity of Judah (and others), Historical Judgment, Historical Redemption, the Messianic Hope, and the Quality of Faith.

1. *The Covenant*

Let me sing for my beloved
a love song concerning his vineyard:
My beloved had a vineyard
on a very fertile hill. . . .

the vineyard of the Lord of hosts
is the house of Israel,
and the men of Judah
are his pleasant planting.

[5:1, 7]

Almost every recorded utterance of the eighth-century prophets (Amos, Hosea, Isaiah, Micah) takes its meaning and relevance from the concept of covenant. It is everywhere presupposed. And yet the specific Hebrew term for covenant, *b*^e*rith* (as in B'nai B'rith="children of the covenant") is not once employed in a passage of undisputed authenticity for *the* covenant between Yahweh and Israel ("Israel" now in the sense in which Isaiah commonly uses it, for the total covenant community).

Why, when the concept of covenant is crucial to all they say, do they apparently deliberately avoid the term? We can only guess that in the eighth century, these four prophets, at least, believed that the term as commonly employed was misused, abused, distorted in meaning. Amos gives us a brilliant example of the diametric difference between popular and prophetic interpretation in what he has to say about the Day of Yahweh (Amos 5:18-20). From Isaiah we read:

> Woe to those . . . who say: "Let him [Yahweh] make haste,
>   let him speed his work
>   that we may see it;
> let the purpose of the Holy One of Israel draw near,
>   and let it come, that we may know it!"
>
> [5:19]

This may well refer to the same Day of Yahweh; and it may at the same time answer our question. In the popular understanding of the covenant, Israel is unqualifiedly guaranteed a happy and speedy issue out of all her difficulties. The prophets apprehend a vaster and more profound covenant purpose and covenant obligation. The covenant will ultimately issue in Yahweh's, not Israel's, glory; and if Israel is oblivious to her own obligations under covenant, she will come under a historical judgment the more severe because of her peculiarly intimate relationship with Yahweh (so Amos 3:2). Isaiah may well have in mind, in part, the popular perversion of the covenant concept when he cries of his own generation:

> They are a rebellious people,
>> lying sons,
>> sons who will not hear
>> the instruction of Yahweh;
>> who say to the seers, "See not";
>> and to the prophets, "Prophesy
>> not to us what is right;
>> speak to us smooth things,
>> prophesy illusions. . . ."
>
> [30:9 f.]

Give us a smooth covenant. Leave us with our illusion that all is well; that Yahweh is ours, and not we his!

Isaiah eschews the term; but he renders the prophetic understanding of the covenant unforgettable in all that he says, and most eloquently, in the Song of the Vineyard (5:1-7). The covenant between Yahweh and Israel is likened to the relationship between a man and his vineyard. When he is lavish in his care of it, it yields not the good grapes he has every right to expect, but, literally (at the end of v. 2) vile-smelling grapes. Now Isaiah drops the third person and speaks for Yahweh in the prophetic first person:

> Judge, I pray you, between me
>> and my vineyard.
> What more was there to do for my vineyard
>> that I have not done in it?

What more could Yahweh do for Israel than he has done? Life, land and possessions she owes to him. And he?

> He looked for justice [*mishpat*],
>> but behold, bloodshed [*mishpah*];
> for righteousness [*sᵉdaqah*],
>> but behold, a cry [*sᵉʾaqah*]!
>
> [5:7]

The "inhabitants of Jerusalem and men of Judah" (v. 3) have themselves vitiated the covenant. And Isaiah defies, as he does repeatedly, the common plea that he speak smooth things. Yahweh will remove his care from this perverse vineyard—nay, he will destroy it!

> I will remove its hedge. . . .
> I will break down its wall. . . .
> I will make it a waste. . . .

This must be; for Yahweh is the Holy One of Israel.

2. The Holiness of Yahweh

> Holy, holy, holy is Yahweh of hosts;
> the whole earth is full of his glory.
> [6:3]
> Yahweh of hosts is exalted in justice [*mishpat*],
> and the Holy God shows himself
> holy in righteousness [*s^edaqah*].
> [5:16, cf. 5:7, quoted above]

The phrase, "the Holy One of Israel" (or of Jacob, or, simply, "the Holy One"), appears some thirty times in the book of Isaiah, and about twelve times in oracles of Isaiah of Jerusalem. Elsewhere in the Old Testament it appears only about ten times, and possibly earlier than Isaiah only once (Hos. 11:9). Yahweh as the Holy One is distinctly and characteristically Isaianic.

What does Isaiah mean to convey by the Holiness of Yahweh? Why do his hearers come at length to cry in exasperation, "Let us hear no more of the Holy One of Israel!" (30:11b)? "Holy" was an ancient term in Canaan, a primitive term long current in fertility religions. The holy was the separate—that which was set apart as pertaining exclusively to the deity. The same Hebrew root was used in the designation of the sacred prostitutes attached to the Canaanite shrines.

Isaiah's characteristic employment of the term represents a phenomenal subsuming and refinement of the primitive idea of holiness. It is common to say that Isaiah gives an ethical content to the term. Obviously he does: justice and righteousness belong to the Holiness of Yahweh (so 5:16, quoted above). But for Isaiah the term embraces vastly more than Yahweh's ethical attributes. Yahweh is holy. Holiness *is* Yahweh. It is that without which Yahweh would be not Yahweh—without which Yahweh would not *be*. The holiness of Yahweh conveys Isaiah's intense practical monotheism: in his call he hears the attendant seraphim (presumably— we are not certain—images of winged creatures with serpentine bodies) praising the holiness of Yahweh as glory filling the whole earth. The covenant is always implicit in the term: it is repeatedly the Holy One *of Israel;* it is for Isaiah as it is put in Hosea (11:9) "the Holy One *in your midst.*" But if holiness is the sum total of deity, it is never deity contemplated mystically, exclusively transcendent, totally "other." Holiness does convey transcendence and otherness but, paradoxically, it forcefully implies at the same time the full impingement of the "Other" upon the life of the world and, with particular purpose in a unique relationship, upon Israel. Martin Buber has aptly called this quality of holiness "radiation."[6] For Isaiah and the prophets there is no god but God-in-life-and-history. Yahweh's holiness alone explains the meaning of existence. As Holy One he is Judge in human history. As Holy One he is also Redeemer.

3. *The Pride and Perversity of Judah*

> Hear, O heavens, and give ear, O earth;
> for Yahweh has spoken:

"Sons have I reared and brought up
but they have rebelled against me.
The ox knows its owner,
and the ass its master's crib;
but Israel does not know,
my people does not understand."

[1:2-3]

They have despised the Holy One of Israel,
they are utterly alienated!

[1:4]

In metered lines, and employing the parallelism characteristic of Hebrew poetry, Isaiah decries the perversity of the covenant people. To allege that this is exclusively or even primarily an ethical protest on the part of the prophet is a woeful misapprehension. The Holiness of Yahweh does involve the divine demand for justice and righteousness; and Isaiah follows Amos in the categorical condemnation of Israel's social sins (see, e.g., 1:16-17, 21-23: 3:14 f.—"grinding the face of the poor"!—and 5:23). Indeed, Isaiah literally damns the total structure of the formal Yahweh cult not for the cult itself but because the ceremonial practice is accompanied, in the grossest hypocrisy, by a corporate life of injustice, oppression and violence. Thus saith Yahweh: "I cannot endure iniquity *and* solemn assembly." [1:13c].

This people draw near with their mouth
and honor me with their lips,
while their hearts are far from me,
and their fear of me is a commandment of
men learned by rote. . . .

[29:13]

Nevertheless, Isaiah clearly understands that social iniquity is only symptomatic of a deep and (as we think Isaiah means it) fatal malignancy. Isaiah sees in Judah a willful and total rebellion of covenant man against covenant God. It is unmitigated, uncompromised, unrelieved—and scandalous —alienation.

> The whole head is sick,
>   and the whole heart faint.
> From the sole of the foot even to the head,
>   there is no soundness in it. . . .
>
> [1:5 f.]

The malignancy is, in a word, pride, and Isaiah repeatedly probes it out in a variety of approaches.

> You turn things upside down!
>   Shall the potter be regarded as the clay;
> that the thing made should say of its maker,
>   "He did not make me";
> or the thing formed say of him who formed it,
>   "He has no understanding"?
>
> [29:16][7]

> Their land [the land of Yahweh's people] is filled
>   with silver and gold,
>   and there is no end to their treasures;
> their land is filled with horses,
>   and there is no end to their chariots.
> Their land is filled with idols;
>   they bow down to the work of their hands,
>   to what their own fingers have made.
>
> [2:7 f.]

> "Woe to the rebellious children," says Yahweh,
> "who carry out a plan, but not mine;
> and who make a league, but not of my spirit. . . ."
>
> [30:1]

All this is covenant man pridefully denying the covenant God—assuming autonomy, creating gods; and putting trust in alliances (Egypt in this case), in a covenant made with *men*.

In one of Isaiah's oracles, his prophetic ire against pride in every form sweeps up for condemnation an astonishing category of objects:

> For Yahweh of hosts has a day
>   against *all* that is proud and lofty,
>   against *all* that is lifted up and high;
> against all the cedars of Lebanon,
>   lofty and lifted up;
>   and against all the oaks of Bashan;
> against all the high mountains,
>   and against all the lofty hills;
> against every high tower,
>   and against every fortified wall;
> against all the ships of Tarshish,
>   and against all the beautiful craft.

But hear the climax!

> And the haughtiness of man shall be humbled,
>   and the pride of men shall be brought low;
>   and Yahweh alone will be exalted in that day.
>   [2:12-17]

We think Isaiah comes very close here to a "doctrine" of man. We are not forgetting what we have called the existential reference—the sharp, specific allusion to the concrete realities of Isaiah's existence; but here, on wings of furious prophetic indignation, Isaiah moves north to Lebanon, west across the Jordan to Bashan, on somewhere, anywhere, to the mountains—and then to the symbols of human pride, the high towers, the fortified cities, and the proud, frail craft that sail the seas. The pride that renders Judah sick unto dying is the more critical because it is shared—by all men!

No, Isaiah would not have *said* this. He approaches, but only approaches, a theological doctrine of man. He does so also when the pride of Assyria is condemned, a pride that says,

> My hand has found like a nest
>   the wealth of the peoples;
> and as men gather eggs that have been forsaken
>   so I have gathered all the earth;
> and there was none that moved a wing,
>   or opened the mouth, or chirped.   [10:14]

Assyria is prey to the same pride, and subject to the same prophetic condemnation. She did not do this by the strength of her own hand, as she boasts (10:13) but as the rod of Yahweh's anger (10:5).

> Shall the ax vaunt itself over him who hews with it,
>   or the saw magnify itself against him who wields it?
> As if a rod should wield him who lifts it,
>   or as if a staff should lift him who is not wood!
>
> [10:15]

If we are not sure how far Isaiah consciously carried his indictment of human pride, we know he saw it as a sickness that would ultimately bring ruin upon Assyria (10:12, 16-18) as well as Judah. Yahweh, Author of the covenant, the Holy One of Israel, visits historical judgment upon human pride and perversity.

4. *Historical Judgment*

> Thus says the Holy One of Israel,
>   "Because you despise this word,

> and trust in oppression and perverseness,
>   and rely on them;
> therefore this iniquity shall be to you
>   like a break in a high wall, bulging out, and
>   about to collapse,
>   whose crash comes suddenly, in an instant;
> and its breaking is like that of a potter's vessel
>   which is smashed so ruthlessly
> that among its fragments not a sherd is found
>   with which to take fire from the hearth,
>   or to dip up water out of the cistern."
>   [30:13]

The city of Jerusalem was twice put to siege during the ministry of Isaiah; first in 735 or 734 by Rezin and Pekah, and again in 701 by Sennacherib. On both occasions Isaiah apparently predicted the lifting of the siege. Of the conspiracy between Syria and Ephraim, Isaiah declared to Ahaz, "Thus says the Lord God: It shall not stand . . . (7:7); and in a recorded oracle already quoted (the authenticity of which has sometimes been questioned), the prophet directs this word of Yahweh to the besieging Assyrians:

> Because you have raged against me
>   and your arrogance has come to my ears,
> I will put my hook in your nose
>   and my bit in your mouth,
> and I will turn you back on the way
>   by which you came.
>   [Isa. 37:29 = II Kings 19:28]

And yet Isaiah, for all that Jerusalem and the Temple meant to him, apparently remained convinced throughout his ministry that judgment would ultimately fall upon Judah and Jerusalem. In the first crisis he confronted Ahaz with a son symbolically named "A remnant shall return"; and he stated an article of faith fundamental to his whole ministry:

If you will not believe,
surely you shall not be established
[7:9b]

Probably shortly after Sennacherib's siege he delivered an oracle to his own people far more severe than that directed against Assyria. The threatened population had not been humbled by that historical chastisement. Bitterly and with finality Isaiah spoke:

In that day the Lord Yahweh of hosts,
called to weeping and mourning,
to baldness and girding with sackcloth;
and behold, joy and gladness,
slaying oxen and killing sheep,
eating flesh and drinking wine. . . .
Yahweh of hosts has revealed himself in my ears:
"Surely this iniquity will not be forgiven you
till you die,"
says the Lord Yahweh of hosts.   [22:12-14]

And as we saw earlier in the present discussion, Isaiah expresses in the account of his call (ch. 6) his conviction that the nation will suffer judgment. "How long, O Lord," he asks—how long will her perversity endure? "Until cities lie waste . . . and Yahweh removes men far away." We observe the probability, of course, that the prophetic word of doom is nearly always implicitly qualified by contingency—that is, the fulfillment of the dire expectation is contingent upon the continuation of the conditions which call it forth. Hope is often implicit in the most passionate prophetic denunciations: in the midst of an extended indictment, Isaiah cries,

Come now, let us reason together,
says Yahweh:
though your sins are like scarlet,
they shall be as white as snow;

> though they are red like crimson,
> they shall become like wool.
> [1:18]

Nevertheless, Isaiah quite apparently believes that the covenant rebellion of the nation—this people, this people of unclean lips—is so obdurate, so deep, so firmly established, so pervertedly *willed* that there will be no turning, no repentance and therefore no redemption until the nation has passed catastrophically under the judgment of Yahweh. So far as the prophet himself is concerned, the contingent possibility of quiet salvation through repentance is an impossible possibility: Israel's redemption, and the ultimate fulfillment of Yahweh's covenant purpose—these lie now only beyond judgment. "If you will not believe, surely you shall not be established" (7:9).

> For thus said the Lord God, the Holy One of Israel,
> "In returning and rest you shall be saved;
> in quietness and in trust shall be your strength."
> And you *would not,* but you said, "No!" [30:15]

5. *Historical Redemption*

> Immanuel = With Us is—God!
> Shear-jashub = A Remnant—will Return!
> Isaiah = Yahweh—Saves!

The final prophetic word is not judgment but redemption. Judgment *is* the wrath of Yahweh, but it is a purposive and constructive wrath, not a vindictive wrath. Judgment is not an end in itself, is not merely punitive. Judgment is the divine extremity to make redemption possible.

> I will turn my hand against you
> and will smelt away your dross. . . .
> and remove all your alloy. [1:25]

In the bitterly controverted "Immanuel" section (7:10-17; see also 8:8) we simply do not know—and cannot know— the identity of the child to be so named. It does not matter: the name is symbolic—With Us is God. It is God who is with us, the Holy One of Israel in our midst. His declared purpose from of old is to bless, through Abraham and Israel, all the families of the earth (see Gen. 12:3, an expression, probably of the faith of the J writer in the tenth century B.C.). It is his purpose in history to redeem, to reconcile rebellious man with himself. But it is God who is with us. It is redemption on his terms—terms which Isaiah understands as quietness, confidence, trust, belief in Yahweh. If Israel will not submit to his terms, then he will bring her to submission in judgment, in fire, in purge. His purpose *will* be fulfilled in history: with us is God!

Only a remnant will survive; but a remnant *will* continue in history, fulfilling the purposes of Yahweh. It is God who is with us. Beyond tragedy there is always hope. It is the nature of God to forgive and redeem. The salvation that Isaiah himself experienced in the symbol of fire, the remnant will know beyond the fire of death and destruction.

Then flew one of the seraphim to me, having in his hand a burning coal which he had taken with tongs from the altar. And he touched my mouth, and said, "Behold, this has touched your lips; your guilt is taken away, and your sin forgiven."

[6:6 f.]

Nearly two centuries later, Isaiah's most distinguished disciple understood his own mission to the survivors of Israel in these terms:

Comfort, comfort my people,
says your God.

> Speak tenderly to Jerusalem,
>> and cry to her
>> that her warfare is ended,
>> that her iniquity is pardoned. . . .
>>> [Isa. 40:1]

As the purged and forgiven Isaiah is charged with a mission to his own nation, so the same disciple sees the purged and forgiven nation charged with a mission to the world:

> It is too light a thing that you should be my servant
>> to raise up the tribes of Jacob
>> and to restore the preserved [the remnant] of Israel;
> I will give you as a light to the nations,
>> that my *salvation* may reach to the end of the earth.
>>> [Isa. 49:6]

Israel (now Judah and Jerusalem) is understood and interpreted in the faith of Isaiah in terms of the covenant relationship with Yahweh, the Holy One of Israel. Her total violation of the covenant in pride and perversity renders her incapable of fulfilling Yahweh's covenant purpose. She will be brought under a tragic divine judgment from which only a remnant will emerge—but a purified remnant, reestablished in the covenant and capable again of glorifying Yahweh. God is with us. A remnant shall return. Yahweh saves.

6. *The Messianic Hope*

Bind up the testimony, seal the teaching among my disciples. I will wait for Yahweh, who is hiding his face from the house of Jacob, and I will hope in him. Behold, I and the children whom Yahweh has given me are signs and portents in Israel from Yahweh of hosts. . . .   [8:16-18]

It is the message of hope and redemption that is sealed, not on lifeless parchment but in the living faith of Isaiah's disciples. The full message of Yahweh's grace, forgiveness and continued covenant activity must await the judgment, lest its proclamation further fatten the already fat hearts and dull the already insensitive faculties of this people. This message in full is released by Second Isaiah in the latter half of the sixth century, following Judah's destruction at the hands of Babylon.

But by one means or another, as we believe, the living seal failed to seal utterly. Isaiah himself may have broken it. Perhaps some of his disciples, earlier than Second Isaiah, were unable for whatever reasons to hold back the message of redemption. In any case we find in the earliest collection of Isaianic material two oracles eloquently proclaiming a redemptive faith. We think 9:2-7 and 11:1-9 are authentic and indeed that the tide of critical judgment against the passages is turning.

We shall not quote them, but we urge their careful rereading, mindful of our discussion here. There is nothing in either incompatible with what we understand elsewhere about the faith of Isaiah. Both are Messianic—that is, simply, both look forward to the coming of a Messiah, an "anointed one." But this projection into the future is in full continuity with the present. Somewhere beyond the judgment of Yahweh upon the nation, the Davidic rule, which Isaiah never protests as such, will be re-established and the covenant purpose fulfilled. This is historical redemption, to be effected by the continuation of Yahweh's mighty deeds—"the zeal of Yahweh of hosts will do this" (9:7)—but in and through and out of the very real exigencies of history. If Isaiah's Messianism has an eschatological flavor, that is, if it anticipates a growing concern in subsequent centuries with the "last things," we may remark that this *is*, for Isaiah, the goal of history; that Isaiah may indeed be the father of Jewish and Christian eschatology; but that for Isaiah it is a "natural" and consistent development of a very real covenant history.

7. *The Quality of Faith*

Isaiah to the king (Hezekiah?):

In that day you looked to the weapons of the house of the forest [Lebanon—the reference is to Judah's arsenal], and you saw that the breaches of the city of David were many, and you collected the waters of the lower pool, and you counted the houses of Jerusalem, and you broke down the houses to fortify the wall. You made a reservoir between the two walls for the water of the old pool. But you did not look to him who did it, or have regard for him [Yahweh] who planned it long ago.   [22:8-11]

For Isaiah, there is only one alternative to frustration, defeat and death, and that is absolute faith in Yahweh. We almost hear him say, He that would save his life must lose it.[8] He does say, If you will not believe you shall not be established. We think Isaiah is misread as a pacifist. Certainly he is misread as a "quietist" if the term connotes the deprecation of human effort. Isaiah never condemns human effort *per se*, but the attitude in which human effort is undertaken. Trust in the work of human hands—any kind of work —is iniquitous when that work is conceived as itself the ultimate end. In the words quoted above, Isaiah says in effect, What you have done is in fact what Yahweh would have had you do, but is it brought to nought because you have put your *faith*, your *trust*, in what you have done and not in him in whose wisdom and for whose purposes all must be done.

And this brings to a head the essential point in the interpretation of the prophets, the so-called ethical prophets. But we can say it better in the categories of social ethics of our own time. In terms, then, of our own time, human effort, social reform, slum clearance, decent wages and working hours and living standards, racial understanding, human brotherhood, world government, adequate medical care, the alleviation of human suffering, the promotion of human rights, the establishment of personal security—all of this, to be sure, we acknowledge as "good" and, hopefully, we work, we expend effort, toward these ends. But if these are ends in themselves—if the "good" society becomes God—then the unqualified prophetic word (right or wrong, and this we are not arguing) pronounces upon them the sentence of damnation. Good in themselves, these efforts become diabolical and doomed to defeat when they are themselves the end, and man is made God. "You did not have regard for him who planned it long ago."

If Isaiah does not say, as a creed of the Christian church puts it, The end of man is to glorify God, he does say with his sharp existential reference to Judah that it is the sole end of covenant man to glorify Yahweh!

We think the faith of Isaiah anticipates remarkably a quality of the faith of Paul, that great Christian apostle to the nations. Paul makes explicit what is always centrally implicit in Isaiah: "Whatever does not proceed from faith is sin" (Rom. 14:23b). This declaration, implicit or explicit, that whatever man does is accursed except it be done to the glory of God appears to us to be either the revelation of God himself or, as some would say, the excretion of a diseased mind.

V. LAW*

Hear, O Israel: The Legal Codes

Hear, O Israel: The Lord our God is one Lord; and you shall love the Lord your God with all your heart, and with all your soul, and with all your might.   DEUT. 6:4 f.

By whatever means, through whatever channels, and to whatever degree, Israel clearly borrowed laws from other Near Eastern cultures. That some of her laws were taken over from the Canaanites cannot be denied. But that Old Testament law was, judged by moral and religious standards, prevailingly on a higher level than that of contemporary and neighboring peoples is also beyond dispute. Bentzen defines the distinction as due to a qualitative difference in religion.[1] Eichrodt puts it more sharply when he speaks of the sincerity and energy with which Israel referred all of her laws to God, in distinction to the shallow formality of the same trait in the laws of other nations.[2] Indeed, the divine reference, explicit or implicit, is so direct and so profound as virtually to erase any real distinction between the sacred and the profane in the Old Testament legal apparatus. Law in the Old Testament is regarded in very fact as the articulation of divine will for the community under covenant.

This is to say, of course, that we deal in the Old Testament with theological law. But can we distinguish more specifically the particular theological presuppositions that

* The material in this chapter appeared in slightly different form in *Interpretation*, Vol. VII, No. 4, October, 1953. Copyright, 1953, by *Interpretation*, and used by permission of the publisher.

give rise to and shape the law? To this end we must first survey, necessarily briefly, the major codes of law in the Old Testament, their superficial characteristics, the general qualities which they hold in common particularly as against other extrabiblical codes, points of difference among the three major earlier codes, the ethical qualities and content of these three, and finally the central theological motivation of all Old Testament law. We may then attempt, from this assessment of the law, to distinguish its primary theological presuppositions.

A. CHARACTERISTICS OF THE MAJOR CODES

The first code of laws in the Old Testament appears in the block of chapters, Exod. 20-23. The first part of 20 (1-17) contains the Ten Commandments, given also in Deut. 5:6-21; and what follows through 23 is generally termed the Covenant Code.[3] Several verses in 22 and 23 having to do with ritual requirements[4] constitute a single code and are closely paralleled in Exod. 34. Both codes are referred to as the Ritual Decalogue.[5] Besides these there are three other major codes: the Deuteronomic Code in Deut. 12-26; the Holiness Code, Lev. 17-26; and the Priestly Code in the rest of Leviticus and in parts of Exodus and Numbers.[6]

Several superficial phenomena are commonly observed. It is interesting to note that according to the multiple-source hypothesis the later documents give increasingly more space to law.[7] J has only the ritual Decalogue in Exod. 34.[8] The E document has only the four chapters in Exodus. D and H, presumably from the seventh and sixth centuries respectively, have a very considerable section; and of course it is law which is the dominant interest of P. Yet such a scheme, regardless of the merits of the now traditional source theories, can be and sometimes has been badly misinterpreted. It does not follow that law and the importance of law in Israel is of relatively late origin. It is increasingly clear that Deuteronomy and the Priestly writings contain at least some material much older than is indicated by the usual dating of the documents.[9] Increasingly, too, it would appear that scholars are disposed to accept the substantial reliability of the persistent tradition which sees Moses as a lawgiver.[10] That law was an early and significant aspect of Israelite culture is further attested not only by ancient Near Eastern parallels but even more strikingly in the life, the work and the character of the first three great names in Israel's national history: Moses, Samuel and Elijah. In all three the types of prophet and priest are combined.

In this connection we may add here briefly a note to which we shall return. The prophetic and the legal are not, as is sometimes alleged, consistently and inimically opposed in the Old Testament. There is, to be sure, a great difference between classical Hebrew prophecy and the ultimate development of legalistic Judaism; but for centuries and beginning with Israel's beginnings prophecy and law developed in close parallel and affinity.

A second obvious phenomenon is that all these major law codes of the Pentateuch are attributed to Moses. To be sure, the priestly point of view sees at least two laws antedating Moses: Sabbath and circumcision; and in later Judaism this tendency grew stronger under the demands of apologetics. Law had been given to all men (as witness the covenant with Noah and the neutral location of Sinai) but only the Jews had observed it.[11] But for the greater span of Old Testament history, Moses was seen as the author, or better, the mediator of law; and as many have pointed out, this unquestionably contributed to the conservative tendency in the handling of the whole legal corpus. Even more significantly, this persistent Mosaic tradition in law also would appear as partially responsible for the high ethical presuppositions which, by and large, pervade the legal framework.

A third characteristic—not unique since it is shared at least superficially by other ancient law codes—is, of course, that all the law is seen as, in very fact, the law of God. God, not Moses, is the author of the law. These are the requirements, not of man, but of God.[12]

Finally, we may note the inseparable relationship of law and covenant. Since virtually all Pentateuchal law is attributed to Moses, it is all seen as stemming originally from the great confederacy bound together under divine covenant at Sinai. If the identification of D with the reform of Josiah is correct, this code represents in the Old Testament a fresh beginning in and a reaffirmation of the Mosaic covenant. And again if tradition is correct, the same is true, much later, in the postexilic community, of the law of Ezra. Examples, early and late, of this inseparable relationship of law and covenant may be cited; such as, the covenant with Abraham in circumcision or, significantly, the prophet Jeremiah and the New Covenant:

This is the covenant which I will make with the house of Israel after those days, says Yahweh: I will put my *law* within them, and I will write it upon their hearts.   [31:33]

While there are inconsistencies in the contents of the various codes of law and while, as we shall see, one code may differ from another in emphasis and in the degree of ethical, social and moral consciousness, there are certain generalities which may be affirmed.

As compared with non-Israelite codes of law, and particularly the Code of Hammurabi, the death penalty is less frequently exacted. There is one notable exception in a series of laws now scattered through Exod. 21 (12, 15-17), 22 (19 f.), and 31 (15b) but thought to be an original and ancient unit, in which series the death penalty is assigned when comparable offenses in other codes are less drastically punished.[13] But the death penalty in these cases serves generally to underline the moral and religious seriousness of the covenant community, and in the Israelite scale it in no wise conflicts with the pattern of law which places human life above all other values save two: the sacredness of family and the integrity of Yahweh.

Israel retained the *Lex Talionis* (Exod. 21:22-25); but while it is harshly in conflict with the measure of mercy evident in much of the later legislation, it clearly represented in an early stage an ethical advance in placing a limit upon damages. And again generally speaking, as compared with other ancient Near Eastern codes of law, brutality in punishment is strikingly absent. Torture is not a weapon of Old Testament law.[14]

Further, the law of Israel knows no class distinctions. Power, whether religious or civil or economic, has no privilege under the law. The slave, of course, remains a slave; but the same judicial principles apply. Indeed, if the law knows any partiality it is toward the weak, the powerless and the dispossessed.

Some have argued for Israelite superiority in laws regulating the relationship of the sexes. This, it seems, is debatable unless one accept *in toto* the circumscribed position of the female in the Hebrew family. But in any case, such laws again reflect the stern moral nature of the Israelite against what appears in contrast as the extreme laxity of the Babylonian or the Canaanite.

If now we compare the Covenant, Deuteronomic and Holiness Codes, accepting them in this conventional chronological order,[15] it is apparent that they reflect in general an increasingly sensitive social and moral conscience and at the same time an increasing interest in cult. The central code of law, largely civil law, in Deut. 12-26 and 28 gives in a considerably expanded and sometimes significantly modified form virtually the full contents of the Book of the Covenant, and in addition a number of laws not paralleled at all in Exod. 20-23. One cannot well escape the conviction that the fundamental difference between the Covenant and Deuteronomic Codes is in very fact the more developed and consistent prophetic note in the later code. Repeatedly and pointedly the older laws of the Covenant Code are restated in Deuteronomy in terms which inescapably suggest the influence of Amos, Hosea and Isaiah. The difference between the two codes may be summarized as follows: (1) Justice is further tempered in behalf of the offender. (2) A still more merciful view is especially pronounced with respect to the weak. The law of Deuteronomy seems methodically to provide legal compensation for those who are victimized by the inequities and brutalities that inhere in the social system. (3) Unmistakably, Deuteronomy reflects in comparison with the Book of the Covenant a deeper and more spiritual religious foundation.

The code of Lev. 17-26 is termed "Holiness" because of its peculiar stress, unparalleled elsewhere in Hebrew law, upon the holiness of Yahweh. As a code, it is even more heterogeneous than the Book of Covenant or Deuteronomy; and much more than either of the other two, it of course strongly emphasizes ritual law. Most strikingly, however, it prescribes with the ritual requirements for meeting the restrictions created by Yahweh's holiness an even higher moral, social and ethical demand than is found in either of the other codes. Yahweh's holiness makes exacting demands in cult and ritual; it also requires a sweeping righteousness in his people. The notable chapter, Lev. 19, often referred to as the highest development of ethics in the Old Testament, begins: "You shall be holy, for I, Yahweh your God am holy"; and for the most part throughout the chapter the terms of holiness are moral and ethical.

There is one other point of interesting distinction among the three codes. After an appropriate introduction relating all laws to God, the Book of the Covenant proceeds to state its laws and regulations for the most part without further reference to the deity, and omitting any clause as to why the law shall be observed or what will result from its infraction (other than the legal penalty) or its observance. Such statements, however, occur frequently in Deuteronomy: "That it may be well with you, and that you may prolong your days"; or "that you do not defile your land"; or "so that you put away the evil. . . . " In Lev. 19 (and less frequently elsewhere in the Holiness Code) the law is concluded with two or three Hebrew words, as a rule: *'ani YHWH*, "I (am) Yahweh," or *'ani YHWH 'elohekem*, "I (am) Yahweh your God."

On the other hand, too much ought not be made of the distinction. In very truth, the fact of divine being is the *raison d'être* of all Old Testament law, whether so stated or not. And it is, in fact, so stated although not in the sharply punctuated fashion of Lev. 19. The Book of the Covenant is in its present form introduced with the Ten Commandments which begin, "I am Yahweh, your God" (Exod. 20:2). And the laws of Deuteronomy are appropriately introduced with the *Sh*e*ma'* (Deut. 6:4), "Hear, O Israel, Yahweh is our God, Yahweh alone."[16]

To point up the nature and disposition of the laws as suggested in what has preceded, we may now briefly summarize their emphatic ethical and social content. To begin with the elemental ethical level, the words of Amos denouncing those who would "make the ephah small and the shekel great, and dealing falsely with balances of deceit" (8:5) are set in formal legal language in both D and H.[17] All three codes under discussion have general laws against the perversion of justice.[18] The principle of sympathy and consideration for the weak is expressed with astonishing variety. There are numerous duplicate and some triplicate laws which buttress the rights of all dependent classes—servants, slaves,[19] captives, the defenseless, the maimed and the handicapped, and of course the poor. Widows, orphans and sojourners, all deprived of the crucial support of intimate male kin, are regarded in the law with full appreciation of this handicap. This is best illustrated in one of the most remarkable single features of the law—its prescribed treatment of the alien. The term in Hebrew, *gēr*, certainly does not apply exclusively to the resident alien, the foreigner in permanent residence, although to be sure this is the sense of Exod. 23:9 (quoted below). Possibly, as Herbert G. May has recently reminded us, the term applies in postexilic times primarily to the resident alien or the proselyte.[20] But that even then this was by no means exclusively the sense is attested by the parallelism of Job. 31:32: "The *gēr* has not lodged in the street; I have opened my doors to the wayfarer." The *gēr* may be a foreigner in permanent or semipermanent residence; but he is also any stranger who happens into the community on a peaceful, friendly and legitimate errand.[21]

This feature of the law is illustrated in Exod. 22:21 and 23:9. Deuteronomy puts it with great vigor as one of the twelve curses in 27:19. In more gentle tones, with a reach of inspired compassion rarely matched in the Old Testament, it occurs again in the Holiness Code, Lev. 19:33 f., and in

Deut. 10:18b f. And the Priestly Code, having apparently in mind primarily the resident alien and potential proselyte, nevertheless specifically defends the equality of the *gēr* before the Lord in Num. 15:14 ff., 29 and 9:14. Perhaps it should be added here that contradictions apparently failed to disturb the Old Testament editorial mind. Like the narrative and prophetic literature, the law has its stated or sharply implied contradictions. For example, and in this connection, Deut. 23:3 declares that neither an Ammonite nor a Moabite shall be permitted to come ceremonially before the Lord. And a foreigner (from a root *nakar* meaning "strange" or "unknown") is sharply distinguished in the law from the *gēr* whose association with the people of the law whether for a longer or shorter time is seen as cordial and constructive. Even where the law distinguished between the home-born and the *gēr*, as it sometimes inconsistently does, this friendly alien fares better than the foreigner, the *ben nekar*. Recall, for example, the statement of Deut. 14:21:

You shall not eat anything that dies of itself; you may *give* it to the *gēr* . . . or you may *sell* it to a foreigner.

For all of this, if one accept the limitations of Israelite law, it is characterized on the whole by a rather phenomenal gentleness of spirit. The well-known and repeated law on gleaning is a case in point, where, incidentally, the *gēr* is especially cited.[22] Indeed, the tenderness of the law reaches even to the lower creatures. Here one recalls the law prohibiting the muzzling of the ox as it treads the grain (Deut. 25:4); the fact that compassion for the work animal is one of the reasons listed for Sabbath observance (Exod. 23:12); the regulation respecting the mother bird and her young (Deut. 22:6 f.); and of course that familiar ancient cult law prohibiting the seething of a kid in its mother's milk (Exod. 23:19).[23]

The principle of compassion is expounded in the law with remarkable variety and flexibility. We have not yet begun to exhaust the sources in which it is directly or indirectly implied, as witness, for example, the law against keeping overnight the garment taken as security (Deut. 24:12 f.); or that against accepting a millstone as a pledge ("for he would be taking a *life* in pledge" [Deut. 24:6]); or even the law prescribing the roof parapet (Deut. 22:8). This last, and many other laws, can easily be grist for the cynic's mill. There is enough of the purely or even shrewdly practical in the law to invite a rebuttal. The *gēr* and the *ben nekar* obviously did provide, in practice, an ambiguity highly convenient for the cruel and the merciless. And, one may repeat, Old Testament laws in their totality are *not* consistently upon a single high moral, ethical and social plane. But on the other hand, one can evaluate and assess the various codes only upon what is clearly the predominant motivation, the usual attitude, the prevailing spirit.

Nowhere does the law of Israel reach such heights as in those laws which attempt to prescribe what one shall be inwardly. The implications for the inward man were hardly lost on the legal mind even in some laws ostensibly regulating only overt conduct; as, for example, the law of Exod. 23:4 f. respecting one's obligation when confronted with one's enemy's straying ox or overburdened ass. Inward motivation is more pronounced in one of the laws cited above:

A *gēr* shall you not oppress; for as for *you* [plural, emphatic], you know the heart [*nephesh*] of a *gēr* because you were *gērim* [plural] in the land of Egypt.

[Exod. 23:9, literally translated]

To love as one loves oneself is of course implicit in this commandment with respect to the *gēr*. It is explicitly formulated, again with the *gēr* as the object, in Lev. 19:34, also cited above: "You shall love him as yourself." And earlier in the same chapter in Leviticus, v. 18, the word "neighbor" is substituted for *gēr* in a context which in penetrating moral sensitivity is quite unsurpassed in the Old Testament:

> You shall not hate your brother in your heart, but you shall reason with your neighbor, lest you bear sin because of him. You shall not take vengeance or bear any grudge against the sons of your own people, but you shall love your neighbor as yourself: I am Yahweh. [Lev. 19:17 f.]

So much, in brief survey, of the ethical quality of three of the major codes—the Covenant Code, the Deuteronomic Code, and the Holiness Code. It is certainly in some measure true that the fire of the free prophetic word is lost in the very attempt to legislate the intrinsically unlegislatable. This is precisely what Jeremiah recognized when he promulgated a new covenant in law written upon the individual heart. There is some evidence that the editors and codifiers of the law themselves were also aware of this. Nevertheless, law though it be, it is in its present form law constructed upon the foundation of prophetic religion.

Now, as the prophets were not primarily motivated, so the law is not *primarily* motivated by the urge to build the good society, or to construct the social vehicle for the proper and appropriate presentation and defense of the dignity of man; not primarily to defend the weak. These are, to be sure, worthy ideals both of the law and of the prophets; but they are in the nature of by-products. This is for the most part law conceived out of the experienced reality of a merciful God, who himself took a victimized nation from among the society of nations and treated it with unparalleled and undeserved gentleness and mercy. It is law that is created and has its being in these words: You shall love the Lord your God with all your heart. This is the essence of the law, an essence eloquently articulated in Deut. 10:12 ff.:

And now, Israel, what does Yahweh your God require of you, but to fear Yahweh your God, to walk in all his ways, to love him, to serve Yahweh your God with all your heart. . . . to Yahweh your God belong heaven and the heaven of heavens, the earth with all that is in it. . . . For Yahweh your God is God of gods, and Lord of lords, the great, the mighty, the terrible God, who is not partial and takes no bribes. He executes justice for the fatherless and the widow, and loves the *gēr*. . . . You shall serve him and cleave to him, and by his name you shall swear. He is your praise; he is your God. . . .

B. LAW AND THE FAITH OF ISRAEL

Having surveyed thus briefly the nature of Old Testament law, and particularly those portions of the law having to do with ethics and morality, we may now ask: What appear to be the central theological presuppositions of the law in its dominant emphases and in the form in which it finally entered the canon? In underlining the fact that Yahweh is both the source and the motivation of the law, the survey above implicitly affirms the general theological unity of law and prophecy; and in distinguishing now three primary presuppositions underlying the law, we submit that, obvious exceptions notwithstanding, the Old Testament literature attains therein a general and significant unity.

Israelite law, in its present total impression, has its deepest roots in the creation faith. We recognize, of course, the relatively late emergence in the Old Testament of a positively and precisely articulated belief in Yahweh's universal creation, and that it is not, indeed, until the time of Second Isaiah that such a belief is taken for granted.[24] On the other hand, the J story of creation in Gen. 2 reflects an early if imprecise creation faith[25] while the eighth-century prophets clearly stand upon a thoroughly practical though untheoretical belief in Yahweh's creative function. In any case, we are concerned here with the presuppositions of Old Testament law in its developed, codified form; and by creation faith we mean not merely the explanation of ultimate origins. We mean rather to suggest by the term three inseparable functions of deity as deity is biblically understood—creation, conservation and transformation;[26] or, in other terms, creation, maintenance and redemption. In the Old Testament, God is known as Creator only because he is first known as Sustainer-Redeemer.[27] The creation faith of the Old Testament nowhere gives the impression that its *primary* interest is in origins as origins; rather is it a faith that speaks from, and back to, historical human existence and in its articulation is concerned to say what man *is* and what in that faith his existence means. The thrust, so to speak, of the creation faith is never toward the past, but directly to the present and, with profound significance, the future.

It is in this sense that we understand the creation faith as it is expressed in Ps. 24, for example:

> The earth is Yahweh's and the fulness thereof
> the world and those who dwell therein.

The profane and the sacred, the civil and the religious, are by and large distinctions which *we* read into the Old Testament. Land, people and property—territory, life and possessions—these are Yahweh's through the indisputable, incontestable right of ownership through creation and conservation.

A second fundamental theological presupposition is in reality the parent of the first. The creation faith is not chronologically primary but is itself derived from the conviction that God acts in history;[28] and this faith in Yahweh's presence and activity in the movement of time and history lends to Israelite law a unique compulsion. The codes insist upon mercy, certainly not for mercy's sake, nor alone because God is by nature merciful; but much more because he has been merciful to us. Mercy it must be because *we know* his mercy. Love the *gēr*, not because you ought to love the *gēr*, or because it makes for peace all around, nor yet alone even because you were once a *gēr;* but much more because you were once a *gēr* befriended and redeemed by Yahweh. As you know God to be out of your own experience in history, so shall you be. And preexilic law, at least, never lost the sense of Yahweh's contemporaneousness, his immediacy in history. This is remarkably illustrated, for example, in the law on defecation (Deut. 23:12 ff.), where the reason for cleanliness is simply stated: "Yahweh your God walks in the camp."

In its matured theology, the Old Testament betrays little consciousness of the order in which it attained its affirmations of faith in history and in creation. Being and event, substance and time, creation and history are equally his. In this faith-full interpretation of existence, Yahweh's claim to ownership through creation and conservation of land, life and substance is never an old claim, but a claim incessantly renewed in historical and timely event. So, consistently, Mosaic law is represented as having a divine validity enhanced by the immediately preceding and freshly experienced encounter with Yahweh in the events of the Exodus. Hence, too, the historical summary in the beginning of Deuteronomy.

Faith in creation and history are joined, in the third basic theological presupposition, by the covenant faith. For the law itself at its own legal level, this is the dominant and most characteristic trait, although obviously it rests upon the interpretation of history in terms of divine activity. If the creation faith has a single primary reference, God; and faith in history a double reference and relationship, God-man; the third, the faith in covenant, is the three-pointed relationship, God-man-man.

Law and covenant are inseparable. The keeping of the law is man's covenant obligation; and while the records pointedly represent Israel's acceptance of covenant as voluntary, they make it equally clear that the nation's redemption—Yahweh's covenant duty—is to be gained in no other way. In the Old Testament faith in creation and history, there can be no other way.[29] From the human side, then, law *is* the covenant, representing Yahweh's requirements for the covenant community respecting both the relationship of man to man and man to God. The covenant, the law, is God's will for the covenant community in its totality. All members of the community are covenant persons, and no part of their activity—none whatsoever—is exempt from covenant obligation. The command, "Love your neighbor as yourself," appears then as an inescapable development of the covenant scheme. Covenant law is law in Yahweh's perspective; and in Yahweh's sight you and your neighbor are essentially the same—both covenant men. So the commandment also to love the *gēr* as oneself. The sojourner too is a covenant man for the length of his sojourn.

It is then, the covenant concept which explains the so-called, one might almost say the mis-called, democratic ideals of the Old Testament. The essence of human *being* is an essence derived from the covenant. The essential quality of life within the covenant community, far outweighing all others, is the covenant quality. The law, then, cannot be partial to power; this is a nonessential and irrevelant distinction. Those whose status is relatively unhappy or unfortunate through no circumstance of their own creation are to receive compensation from the law and the community: they are covenant persons. And in the final word, of course, no one is exempt from covenant definition, not even the king.[80] The influence of the covenant concept upon the ideal structure of the community is illustrated in the Decalogue, which rests upon and is unified by the covenant principle: its negatives are an effort to guarantee with a minimum a community in which the man-man relationship and the man-God relationship conform to Yahweh's will. Man will find the fulfillment of his life, and participation in true community, when his only object of worship is God, and when he and his fellows hold in mutual inviolable respect the totality of the neighbors' life.[31]

C. THE PRIESTLY LEGISLATION AND YAHWEH'S MERCY

While postexilic priestly law appears to be increasingly concerned with ritual—a concern perhaps inescapably induced by general environmental and ideological changes—it is essential to remember that *all* of the major codes of law in the Old Testament were preserved, transmitted, and of course edited, by the postexilic priests who, in the very act of incorporating so-called prophetic law in the total legal corpus, place their approval upon it.

In a more austere and formalized concept, the creation faith was retained and given magnificent expression in the first chapter of Genesis. With undiminished significance, the faith in creation also underlies the later priestly legislation. With respect to the second theological presupposition of the earlier codes, faith in the Yahweh of history, there can be no doubt that much of the vigor and vividness of the concept is lost. God's historical activity tends increasingly to be seen as a kind of past dispensation; and the presence of God in the congregation both past and contemporary is represented with an increasingly numinous aspect. It is the covenant faith that appears to be most seriously modified, although again one must bear in mind the fact that the Holiness Code, for example, was incorporated with editorial additions in an otherwise consistently legalistic priestly writing. But in cult-centered law, the relationship is no longer the God-man-man pattern of prophetic law, but must now be put in the pattern God-man-God. And yet, concern for the faithful community, for the persons in its devoted membership, is undiminished. Postexilic law just as ardently sought the well-being, the fulfillment, the salvation of the community as did the earlier law. But the dual emphasis has given way to a single primary stress: fulfillment lies in consuming devotion to cult and ritual. Yet we are justified in assuming that to the priestly mind the righteous relationship of man and neighbor was already sufficiently stressed in legal tradition and would inevitably follow (insofar as it could) the keeping of the ritual law.

If the later legislation thus modifies and narrows the covenant faith, at the same time and for the same reasons it adds to the concept a new dimension and suggests again that legalism's silence on social issues is by no means indifference but rather a sober and deeply concerned pessimism. Malachi, probably to be dated in the first half of the fifth century B.C., is written by a man who stands between the era of legalism and the older epoch dominated by the prophet. Mal. 2:10 asks the question which introduces the new dimension; and it is interesting to note that the question is itself preceded by two rhetorical questions which at once are addressed to and define the covenant community: "Have we not all one father? Has not one God created us?" Then—

and this is the question thrown out in anguish—"Why then are we faithless to one another, profaning the covenant of our fathers?" Postexilic priestly symbolism sharply underlines the sense of the centrality of sin, and certainly it cannot be exclusively cult sins. In the priestly writings, the holiest symbol, above all other holy, is the mercy seat. It is the footstool of God, the most sacred symbol within the veil, within the Holy-of-Holies. At the center of the center, the nucleus of the nucleus—the seat of God's *mercy.*

Lev. 16 describes the appropriate rites to be observed on the Day of Atonement. Details of the postexilic observance wanting here may be filled in from the tractate "Yoma" in the *Mishnah,* where the prayer of the priest, pronounced with his two hands upon the scapegoat, is given as follows:

O God, thy people, the House of Israel, have committed iniquity, transgressed, and sinned before thee. O God, forgive, I pray, the iniquities and transgressions and sins which thy people, the House of Israel, have committed and transgressed and sinned before thee. . . . [32]

At various points throughout the ceremony the people gave a response: "Blessed be the name of the glory of his kingdom for ever and ever." The goat was then taken to a place called Zok, about twelve miles from Jerusalem. The people followed in sober procession; and arriving there, the goat was pushed backward off the edge of a cliff.[33] So, too, in Lev. 16 (whatever the interpretation of Azazel) the symbolism is at least in part that of the complete penitence for sin and God's equally complete removal of sin.

> As far as the East is from the west,
>> so far has he removed our transgressions from us.[34]

Guilt is gone. This is transformation. This is redemption. It is in a sense redemption achieved through the grace of

God, a mediated grace, grace—if the term may be used—that is given through the efficacious cult, the effective and appropriate ceremony and ritual. Purification, justification, redemption—this is the gift of God claimed in the priestly prescriptions.

Old Testament law in its totality results from the influence both of prophecy and priesthood, and the two are hardly so disparate as is sometimes alleged. Underlying both schemes are the presuppositions that the God who is present and acts in history is also the God of creation. And for both, albeit with differing interpretation and emphasis on covenant obligation, the believing community is in process of purification and redemption, for the ultimate fulfillment of Yahweh's covenant purpose.

Notes

Introduction

[1] Norman H. Snaith, *The Distinctive Ideas of the Old Testament* (Philadelphia: Westminster Press, 1946), p. 14.

[2] *The Clarendon Bible*, Vol. VI (Oxford: Clarendon Press, 1947), p. vii.

[3] Robert H. Pfeiffer, *Introduction to the Old Testament* (New York: Harper & Brothers, 1941), p. 260.

[4] See Chap. IV, pp. 172 ff.

[5] Graf and Wellhausen were distinguished and highly influential German scholars of the nineteenth century.

[6] *Introduction to the Old Testament* (Copenhagen: G. E. C. Gad, 2nd ed., 1952), Vol. II, p. 24.

Chapter I. *Myth*

[1] See further Pfeiffer, *op. cit.*, pp. 192 ff.

[2] This frequently proposed rendering of the Hebrew is accepted by Gerhard von Rad as syntactically possible, that is, as a valid alternative translation to the more common rendering (so R.S.V.) "In the beginning God created the heavens and the earth. The earth was" etc. But Professor von Rad rejects on theological grounds our rendering here in favor of the more conventional reading. Always predisposed to follow von Rad, I fail to see the cogency of his argument here. See his *Das Erste Buch Mose* in the series *Das Alte Testament Deutsch* (Göttingen: Vandenhoeck and Ruprecht, 1952 f.), pp. 36 f.

[3] For a detailed discussion of the cosmogony of Genesis, see S. R. Driver, *The Book of Genesis* (London: Methuen and Co., 1909), pp. 19 ff.

[4] A full discussion of the Israelite concept and vocabulary of time will be found in H. Wheeler Robinson, *Inspiration and Revelation in the Old Testament* (Oxford: Clarendon Press, 1946), pp. 106 ff.

[5] See Edwyn Bevan's tribute to the P account of creation in S. H. Hooke, *In the Beginning*, The Clarendon Bible, Vol. VI (Oxford: Clarendon Press, 1947), pp. 160 f.

[6] Hooke, *op. cit.*, pp. 38 ff.

[7] For a concise enumeration of these reasons, see *A Commentary on the Bible*, ed. A. S. Peake (Edinburgh: Thomas Nelson and Sons, Ltd., 1937), p. 143.

[8] For a discussion of, and significant quotations from, the Babylonian story from which our accounts are drawn see Driver, *op. cit.*, pp. 103 ff., or John Skinner, *Genesis*, International Critical Commentary (Edinburgh: T. and T. Clark, 1930), pp. 175 ff.; or, for a briefer comparison, *Interpreter's Bible*, Vol. I (Nashville and New York: Abingdon Press, 1951), pp. 450 f.

9 See Norman H. Snaith, *The Distinctive Ideas of the Old Testament* (Philadelphia: Westminster Press, 1946), p. 14.

10 Here, and in my general interpretation of Genesis, I am indebted to Professor Gerhard von Rad, not only for his commentary on Genesis, already cited, but also for his Heidelberg lectures on the Theology of the Hexateuch in the summer of 1953 and the fall and winter, 1954-55.

11 Peake, ed., *op. cit.*, p. 142.

Chapter II. *Legend*

1 The Hittite kingdom flourished, in what is now Turkey, during the middle centuries of the second millennium B.C. We are indebted here to Professor G. D. Mendenhall in a paper presented before the Old Testament Colloquium, Fall, 1953.

2 The problem of terminology is particularly acute here. Neither of the two sections of Genesis is consistent: both now comprise varied literary material. For example, Gen. 1 is totally different from Gen. 2, and Gen. 24 from Gen. 28. And the term "myth" is especially difficult. I use it for want of a better term, intentionally implying an ultimate mythological background for much of the material in Gen. 1-11, but recognizing at the same time the thoroughgoing way in which Israel "historicized" all of her myths. See further Arthur Weisser, *Glaube und Geschichte im Alten Testament*, Kohlhammer, Stuttgart, 1931, pp. 23 ff.

3 Here I must make particular acknowledgment of von Rad's *Das Erste Buch Mose*, cited in Chapter I. Readers familiar with that work will recognize both the dependence upon, and the departure from, von Rad's interpretation.

4 The classification of legend follows in general that of Hermann Gunkel (tr. W. H. Carruth), *The Legends of Genesis* (Chicago: The Open Court Publishing Co., 1901).

5 For a detailed discussion of the E document, see any standard Introduction.

6 So, also, Robert C. Dentan, "The Unity of the Old Testament," *Interpretation*, Vol. V, No. 2 (April, 1951), especially p. 164.

7 So von Rad, *op. cit.*, p. 29.

8 W. F. Albright, *The Biblical Period* (Pittsburgh, 1950), p. 7, reprinted from *The Jews; Their History, Culture, and Religion* (New York: Harper & Brothers, 1949), ed. Louis Finkelstein.

9 See Millar Burrows, *An Outline of Biblical Theology* (Philadelphia: Westminster Press, 1946), pp. 295 f.

10 And see also David Daube, *Studies in Biblical Law* (Cambridge: The University Press, 1947).

11 Albright, *op. cit.*, p. 7.

12 Von Rad, *op. cit.*, pp. 27 f.

13 Dentan, *loc. cit.*

14 *Op. cit.*, p. 32.

Chapter III. *History*

1 E.g., Pfeiffer, *op. cit.*, pp. 340 ff.

2 As discussed by R. G. Collingwood, *The Idea of History* (Oxford: The Clarendon Press, 1946), p. 24.

3 In support of this view see John Bright, *The Kingdom of God* (Nashville and New York: Abingdon Press, 1953), p. 33, n. 24.

⁴ See further von Rad, *op. cit.*, pp. 8 ff.

⁵ See the extended footnote in T. H. Robinson, *A History of Israel*, Vol. I (Oxford: The Clarendon Press, 1932), pp. 287 f.

⁶ The present text is unsatisfactory. See T. H. Robinson, *op. cit.*, pp. 215 f.

⁷ See Albright, *op. cit.*, p. 25.

⁸ Pfeiffer, *op. cit.*, p. 341.

⁹ From "The Rock," *Collected Poems*, by T. S. Eliot, p. 188. Copyright, 1934, by Harcourt, Brace & Co. Used by permission of Harcourt, Brace & Co., and Faber & Faber, Ltd.

¹⁰ We are in substantial agreement with the interpretation of T. H. Robinson, *op. cit.*, pp. 239 ff.

¹¹ See R. H. Pfeiffer, "Facts and Faith in Biblical History," *Journal of Biblical Literature* Vol. 70, no. 1 (March, 1951), p. 5.

¹² The text of I Kings 6 is obscure at points and an exact reconstruction of the temple is hardly possible, although many have attempted it. Ezekiel's description of the restored temple in Ezek. 40-48 and Josephus' detailed outline of Herod's temple are of some help. Perhaps the most satisfactory attempt at reconstruction is that of Garber and Howland: see "Reconstructing Solomon's Temple" by Paul L. Garber, *The Biblical Archaeologist*, Vol. xiv, no. 1 (Feb., 1951).

¹³ Fertility symbols apparently adorned the temple in profusion (see I Kings 6:29). Around the outside of the temple side chambers were built, for what purpose we do not precisely know. At times they may have been used for representations or images of other deities. Solomon himself certainly made provision for the worship of many other gods than Yahweh.

Chapter IV. *Prophecy*

¹ This, and all subsequent dates in this chapter, are after Albright, *op. cit.*, pp. 29 ff.

² *Ibid.*, pp. 39 f.

³ The introductory formula (supplied by the Deuteronomic editors of Kings) usually correlates the reign of the king in question with that of the ruling king in the sister kingdom (see, e.g., I Kings 15:1 and 15:25). This exclusively internal synchronism makes absolute dating difficult if not impossible. In most instances, scholars have been able only to approximate the dates of accession and death. For a discussion of the nature of the problem, see T. H. Robinson, *op. cit.*, "The Chronology of the Regal Period," pp. 454 ff.

⁴ For treatment of the literary problem of Isaiah, see Peake (ed.), *op. cit.*, p. 436; more exhaustively Pfeiffer, *op. cit.*, pp. 416-21; more conservatively, with the literary problem placed sensitively in the context of theology and history, John Bright, *The Kingdom of God* (Nashville and New York: Abingdon Press, 1953), pp. 71 ff.

⁵ Isa. 8:16; and see Martin Buber (tr. Carlyle Witton-Davies, from the Hebrew), *The Prophetic Faith* (New York: Macmillan, 1949), pp. 147 and 202 ff. Aage Bentzen also speaks of Isaiah's "circle of disciples" in *Introduction to the Old Testament* (Copenhagen: G. E. C. Gad, 2nd, two-vol. ed., 1952), II, p. 108.

⁶ *Op. cit.*, p. 136.

⁷ Some scholars question the authenticity of this passage. Granting that the verses which immediately follow (Isa. 29:17-24 are probably "of Deutero-

Isaianic milieu" (Buber, *op. cit.*, p. 208), the case against 29:16 is, in my judgment, quite inconclusive.

8 Mark 8:35, Matt. 10:39, Luke 9:24; cf. John 12:25.

Chapter V. *Law*

1 *Op. cit.*, p. 219.

2 W. Eichrodt, *Theologie des Alten Testaments* (Leipzig: J. C. Hinrich, Vol. I, 1938), p. 28. Cf. the following statement by Gunnar Ostborn, in *Tora in the Old Testament* (Lund: H. Ohlssons, 1945), p. 149: "If we now ask . . . what is the particular characteristic of Israelite religion in this respect [ethics], the answer would appear to be that it is precisely the energy and consistency with which the moral issue is harped upon in the religions of the OT which constitutes its distinguishing factor, as against the analogous utterances to be found in other oriental religions."

3 the section 23:20-33 is commonly regarded as an appendix.

4 22:29b-30 and 23:12, 14, 19.

5 The form in Exod. 22-23 is generally regarded as earlier, in part on the grounds that 22:29b still requires human sacrifice.

6 This totals six codes. Pfeiffer, *op. cit.*, p. 210, adds a seventh, the Twelve Curses of Deut. 27:14-26; and one might of course include Ezek. 40-48 as being somewhat in the category of law.

7 Since for our purposes here the question is not of crucial moment, we shall accept in general, as we have in the preceding essays, the now conventional view of the entity and relative dating of the documents in the order J, E, D, H, P, recognizing with Bentzen, *op. cit.*, Vol. II, p. 23, that "the present situation concerning the question of the Pentateuch . . . is rather in suspense. Especially among scholars of the younger generation there exists a definite skepticism towards the Documentary Hypothesis."

8 Its inclusion in the J document is questioned by some scholars.

9 See, e.g., Bentzen, *op. cit.*, Vol. II, pp. 62 ff.

10 Bentzen, *op. cit.*, Vol. I, p. 218.

11 See G. F. Moore, *Judaism* (Cambridge: Harvard University Press, 1927), Vol. I, pp. 274 ff.

12 Daube, *op. cit.*, apparently doubts the accuracy of this general interpretation. "Why we should infer . . . that law sprang from religion rather than that religion sprang from law, it is hard to see" (p. 3). Daube does agree, however, that in its present form the Old Testament represents all law as of divine origin; so pp. 1 f.

13 And in Deuteronomy adultery, 22:22-27, man-stealing, 24:7, and obstinate disobedience of parents, 21:18-21, all receive the death penalty with, of course, murder, 19:11 ff. For Deuteronomy, the most heinous offense, always punishable by death, is idolatry, the worship of other gods.

14 With overtones remarkably revealing of the concept of community, this is illustrated in the law, Deut. 25:2 f., limiting stripes to forty in number and stipulating that they be applied in the presence of the judge. No more than forty, because the punished man will lose his rightful status of dignity and respect in the community.

15 See above, note 7 in this Chapter. Precise dating of the major documents in their present form is impossible. All incorporate older material and in varying degree all have suffered later intrusion and revision. Conventionally,

they have been dated in the order Covenant (ninth century), Deuteronomic (seventh), Holiness (sixth), and Priestly (fifth). See the Introductions.

[16] Or, as the English versions, "Yahweh our God is one Yahweh."

[17] Deut. 25:13 ff. and Lev. 19:35 ff.

[18] Exod. 23:1 ff., Deut. 16:19 ff., and Lev. 19:15.

[19] See, for example, the increasingly sensitive and generous legal provisions for the Hebrew slave, Exod. 21:2, Deut. 15:12 ff. and Lev. 25:39.

[20] *Journal of Biblical Literature*, xvi, no. 2, pp. 100 f.

[21] See J. Pedersen, *Israel*, Vol. I-II (London: Oxford University Press, 1926), p. 40.

[22] See Deut. 24:19 ff. and Lev. 19:9 f.

[23] Cf. Lev. 22:28. But many would question any element of compassion in this old taboo.

[24] Isa. 40:26 and 44:24. Cf. H. Wheeler Robinson, *op. cit.*, p. 22.

[25] O. Procksch, *Die Genesis* (Leipzig: Deichert, 1924), p. 19; and on the antiquity of the faith in creation, see also Eichrodt, *op. cit.*, Vol. II, p. 47.

[26] The terms are Robinson's, *op. cit.*, pp. 17 ff.

[27] See Eichrodt, *op. cit.*, Vol. II, pp. 49 ff. Cf. also my discussion in Chap. I, above.

[28] Eichrodt, *op. cit.*, Vol. II, pp. 48 ff.

[29] See Deut. 30:15 ff.

[30] So Deut. 17:18 ff.

[31] Cf. Pedersen, *op. cit.*, p. 354.

[32] "Yoma" vi 2, tr. by H. Danby, *The Mishnah* (New Haven: University Press, 1933), p. 169.

[33] *Ibid.*

[34] Ps. 103:12.

Index

"A" source of Samuel and Kings, 109, 110, 118
Abel; *see* Cain-Abel story
Abiathar, 126, 140, 142, 145, 146
Abigail, 120, 127
Abigail (David's sister), 143
Abishai, 141, 143, 144
Abner, 122, 128-29, 140, 143, 144
Abraham, xvii, 60-71, 72, 73, 77, 79, 80, 81, 83, 88, 195
  compared with Noah, 62
  covenant of God with, 37, 38, 60-61, 63-64, 65-70
  and history of Israel, 101-3, 104, 105
Absalom, 133, 135-41
Achish of Gath, 125, 127
Adonijah, 145
Adoniram, 152
Ahab, 158
Ahaz, 156, 162, 171, 173, 184
Ahaziah, 159
Ahijah, 154
Ahimaaz, 141
Ahithophel, 138, 140
Alien, treatment of, 199-200, 201-2, 205, 206
Amalekites, 73, 127
Amasa, 142, 143
Amaziah, 160
Ammon, 95, 160
Amnon, 135-36
Amorites, 72
Amos, 170, 175, 176, 180, 197, 199
Amoz, 170, 171
Animals, compassion for, 200-1
Archaeological discoveries, 63, 72-73, 99, 160
Aristotle, 108
Ark of the covenant, 129, 139-40
Asa, 158
Asahel, 128, 143

Asceticism, absence of, 26
Ashdod, 164, 165
Asherah, 158
Assyria, 161-62, 163, 164-66, 171, 183
Astruc, 34
Athaliah, 158-59
Atonement, Day of, 209
Azariah, 160-61

"B" source of Samuel and Kings, 109, 110, 118
Babel story, 44, 52-56, 154
Barzillai, 142
Bathsheba, 133, 135, 145, 146
Beersheba, 71
Benjamin, 93, 94
Bentzen, Aage, xxii, 192
Bethel, 71, 86, 87, 89, 94
Bible; *see also* Old Testament
  interpretation of, xiii-xiv, 34-42
  rediscovery of, xiii
Buber, Martin, 179

Cain-Abel story, 43, 45, 46-48, 55, 57, 133, 154
Canaan, Israel's claim to, 88, 95
"Charismatic" quality, 116, 118, 122-23 124
Chronicles, history of David in, 130
Circumcision, 64, 79, 194, 195
Class distinctions, absence of, 196
Consummation, theme of, xvii
Context, interpretation in light of, 44, 51-52
Covenant of God and man, 52, 60-61, 63-64, 65-70, 81, 86, 104
  and the law, 195, 205-7
  New, 195, 202
  as prophetic theme, 175-78
Covenant Code, 193, 196-202
Covenant faith, xvii, 61-62, 63, 66, 68, 69, 70, 205-7, 208

217